St Hilary

A history of the place and its people

St Hilary

A history of the place and its people

by

Hilary M. Thomas

ST HILARY 2000

The grant from the Heritage Lottery Fund
towards the publication of this book
is gratefully acknowledged.

ISBN: 0-9537804-0-6

Published by St Hilary 2000

Designed and produced in Wales by:
Keith Brown & Sons Ltd.,
Cowbridge.

CONTENTS

LIST OF ILLUSTRATIONS

Small unnumbered details:

Endpapers:

PREFACE

I have lived for five years in St Hilary in a farmhouse that is reputed to have been constructed *c.*1540. It had been tenanted until 1966 and I have met every occupier (or their direct descendants) of the house since 1904. I knew that the village hall had been the school and could picture in my mind's eye the children in Victorian dress sitting at their desks. I knew not a great deal more about the village's history.

After reading Hilary Thomas' *St Hilary. A History of the place and its people*, I am now more fascinated than ever, for I am able to picture the village not just one hundred years ago but many centuries earlier. Hilary's dedicated research, following on from her work in the Glamorgan Record Office and her numerous local history publications, is presented in a style that stimulates interest and is so 'readable'.

As a result of reading the book, I now know that one of the most photographed 'traditional' old thatched cottages in the Vale of Glamorgan was in fact only built in the 1950s. The village's agricultural links are well known but what about its once thriving lead mines?

Twelve years ago I was one of the founders of 'Pride in Barry', an organisation which was set up to stimulate a necessary improvement in the community spirit in that town. When I came to live in St Hilary the contrast could not have been more marked. Here was a small village which by its own endeavours ran the church, the village hall and a thriving Women's Institute and had a community focus in the Bush inn. Celebrations to mark the village's medieval origins had taken place in 1990 and four years later villagers were still enjoying talking about the events.

In January 1997 a meeting of villagers was held and it was decided to celebrate the coming millennium. 'St. Hilary 2000' was born. Since then 'St. Hilary 2000' has organised a feast of events, some primarily for fund raising others for social purposes, which has had the effect of stimulating the already fine community spirit. It also decided that some mark should be left to show our presence here at this time and something of tangible benefit for future generations.

Two major projects have been undertaken, the compilation of this history and the addition of a sixth bell to those already in the church tower. Appropriately, the new treble bell bears the inscription *To the Glory of God. The St Hilary 2000 Community Jubilee Bell.*

Every year the village is invaded by primary schoolchildren from the schools in the Vale of Glamorgan and Cardiff who come to study the history and geography of the village as part their national school curriculum. To help them in their studies, a copy of this book is being given to every primary school in these areas. On behalf of the 'St Hilary 2000' Committee, I acknowledge with gratitude the grant from the Heritage Lottery Fund which has made this gift possible.

A young talented villager, Simon Williams, has kindly designed the dust jacket and we are all grateful to him. However, the outstanding generosity of Hilary Thomas in researching, writing and preparing this publication leaves us in awe. All villagers wish to record their heartfelt gratitude, for we all know that without Hilary this book would not have been possible. We are proud to have considered her an honorary villager for many years.

It is hoped that all villagers and visitors will find this history both fascinating and enjoyable.

Michael Kemp
Chairman - St Hilary 2000

FOREWORD

Standing at the threshold of a new millennium, what is more natural than to look back over the last thousand years to its dawning and to scan the ensuing course of events? It is therefore apt that a work which charts the history of St Hilary over the last millennium should be published now as part of the community's new millennium celebrations. Such books allow us to feel our past, glimpse our forebears and take pride in firmly anchored roots. Such sentiments also underlie the Wales Tourist Board's 'Homecoming 2000' programme designed to attract people with Welsh connections living overseas to return to Wales, to tap into their roots and to revitalise family ties and friendships.

The author of *St Hilary. A History of the place and its people*, Hilary M. Thomas, who I am assured is no relation of the saint, also presents the reader with a mystery. The dedication to Saint Hilary, a fourth-century bishop of Poitiers, is unique in the Vale of Glamorgan and is indeed rare throughout the British Isles. Could there have been an earlier church dedicated perhaps to one of the popular Celtic saints, such as Teilo or Cadoc? Indeed, could there have been a thriving church and community before the coming of the Normans? These questions are, for the present, unanswerable. So far, there are no vestiges of village life pre-dating the second millennium at St Hilary. This does not mean that the community did not exist earlier, nor render the history any less fascinating.

Local histories can do much in practical terms. As chairman of the Wales Tourist Board I appreciate how attractive they can be to the overseas visitor, particularly one whose ancestors might hail from the area. In many ways these documents complement the work of the Board. They particularise part of our message. They show how the myths and legends weave the fabric backing the richly embroidered tapestry that is the true history of Wales. They are an example of local pride and local enterprise, giving visitors a feel for the land they have entered, enabling them to interpret the natural and built environment and to glean insights into the way of life and culture of the local populace. It is fitting, then, that St Hilary should be a major feature in the integrated history/geography curriculum in Cardiff's schools.

Such readable histories also say, indirectly, much about the existing community—its attraction for the visitor, its dynamism, and its sense of identity and of place in geography and time. Such is the value of *St Hilary. A History of the place and its people*. I therefore commend to you, the reader, this brightly-hued, silken knot in the tapestry of Welsh history.

Tony Lewis
January, 2000

1. St Hilary and the Vale, 1578.
(Detail from Christopher Saxton's map of the county of Glamorgan.)

INTRODUCTION

The first thousand years of the Christian era, years which encompassed Roman occupation, the so-called Dark Ages and the Age of the Saints, have left enduring legacies in the Vale of Glamorgan. A Roman villa has been discovered at Llantwit Major, evidence of Roman settlement has been found at Cowbridge, sections of the Roman road, the medieval Portway, still mark the northern edge of the coastal lowlands. It is known that, in the centuries following the departure of the Romans from Britain, Celtic Christianity flourished in the great monastic centres at Llancarfan and Llantwit Major (where a fine series of early Christian monuments still survive), and that from these centres of spirituality and learning the Christian message was spread by the foundation of small daughter churches to serve the needs of local communities.

The village of St Hilary stands on the southern edge of Stalling Down and St Hilary Down, close to the old Roman road, and from its elevated plateau commands a panoramic view of the Vale's coastal plain to the sea. Cottages and houses, some of considerable antiquity, cluster around the medieval church. The parish is bounded on its western edge by the river Thaw and lies at the heart of the fertile Vale. But when did settlement first take place in this favoured and strategic location? The question remains unanswered, for no ancient earthworks have been discovered here, no evidence of Roman settlement, no early Christian monuments, nothing in fact to indicate that St Hilary existed in the first millennium. Only in the wake of the Anglo-Norman incursions into South Wales in the late-eleventh century does the history of village and parish begin to emerge.

This book traces the history of St Hilary from the Middle Ages to the twentieth century. It has been compiled to celebrate the past and to mark the dawn of a new millennium, the history of which has yet to unfold, and is, necessarily, an incomplete and highly selective compilation. What is attempted here is a portrayal of the character of the place and its people, insights into some of the events and personalities, from the significant to the 'ordinary', which have given village and parish a particular identity.

2. A view of the village, 1998.

Saint Hilary
depicted in a stained-glass window in the church.

THE CHURCH FROM THE MIDDLE AGES TO THE REFORMATION

The first recorded reference to the church and by implication to the place, is found in a document dated 1119, although church and community were probably established here considerably earlier. In that document Bishop Urban of Llandaff claimed St Hilary church among the possessions of his see, and thereafter it remained firmly in the hands of the Cathedral and its Chapter.

Few churches in the British Isles are dedicated to Saint Hilary, a fourth-century bishop of Poitiers and champion of Christian orthodoxy, and only two parishes in the country bear that name—St Hilary in Cornwall and St Hilary in the Vale of Glamorgan. On the Continent the dedication is more common, and until recent times it was assumed that the Vale church was founded by the Normans as they 'conquered' Glamorgan at the end of the eleventh century. Scholars now suggest that there was a pre-Norman church on or near the site of the present building and that its dedication to a continental saint is entirely consistent with the spread of influences from Europe long before the Norman incursions. It is also suggested that St Hilary may have been one of the daughter churches within the large territorial area of the old monastic or *clas* church of Llancarfan. But all that can be said with certainty is that *ecclesia Sancti Ylarii* [the church of St Hilary] was in existence in 1119, and that by that date it was serving the needs of a local community.

If indeed a pre-Norman church ever existed in St Hilary no trace of such a structure has survived. The earliest architectural features in the present church date from the twelfth or thirteenth century, since which time both the fabric and the contents of the building have undergone many changes. Rebuilding may have taken place in the 1230s, for in 1229, as recorded in the Margam Annals, the rebellious Welsh 'namely the men of Hywel ap Maredudd [lord of Miskin], burnt the vill of St Nicholas and the vill of St Hilary'.

3. St Hilary church (photographed 1998).

The church in its earliest form would have comprised simply nave and chancel, the south aisle and porch being added in the fourteenth century and the tower a little later. Survivals from the medieval building include the external stone walls and, within the church, the slightly pointed chancel arch, the five steps in the thickness of the north wall of the nave which led to the rood loft, and the two small windows which illuminated the rood and its stair. The massive cylindrical stone font and the hexagonal holy-water stoup are also medieval in date, as are the consecration crosses above windows in the chancel and south aisle, and the priest's door in the south wall of the chancel.

Font

Stoup

Rood loft stairs

4. Medieval survivals in the church.

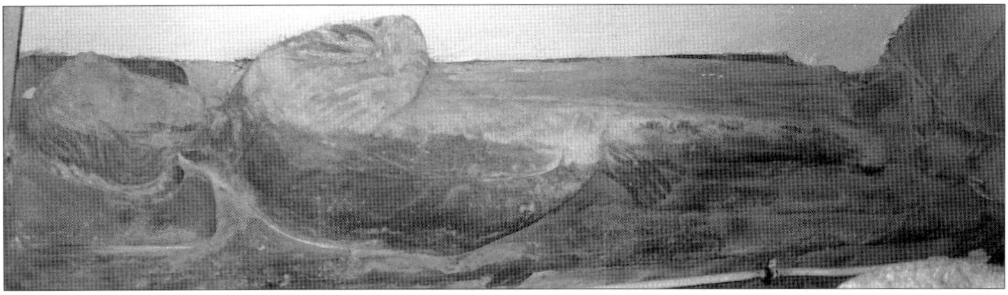

5. Effigy of civilian believed to be a member of the de Cardiff family.

Two monumental effigies in the church also provide links with the medieval church and community. One, lying in a niche in the north wall of the nave, represents a young man in civilian dress and is believed to be that of a member of the de Cardiff family, lords of the manor of St Hilary in the twelfth and thirteenth centuries. The other, that of a knight in full armour, commemorates Thomas Basset of Beaupre who died in 1423. Originally placed within the chancel rails, the Basset tomb-chest with its effigy is now sited in the central part of the church.

Although the essential structural form of the church has altered little since it was first built, the medieval church would have presented a very different appearance to its congregation from that seen today. Externally it would have been white, its stonework covered with regular overlays of limewash. The building may at one time have been thatched, more probably roofed with stone tiles. Internally, wall paintings (such as survive at Llantwit Major and Colwinston), images of saints, a rood surmounted with the figure of the crucified Christ, ornaments and vestments both instructed and awed the congregation. And the mystery of the mass would have been underlined by the priest chanting, in latin, in the seclusion of the sanctuary. Few names of the priests who celebrated the mass and ministered to the spiritual needs of their congregation at St Hilary in the centuries before the Reformation are known, and the impact of the Reformation on this small community can only be guessed at.

By the Act of Supremacy, which declared King Henry VIII and his heirs to be 'the only supreme head in earth of the church called Ecclesia Anglicana', papal authority was transferred to the Crown and the centuries-old bonds with Rome were broken. Clergy throughout England and Wales were now required to swear an oath of loyalty to the new Supreme Head, and Laurence Thomas, vicar of St Hilary in 1534, would have been one of those summoned to Llandaff to take the oath.

6. Effigy of Thomas Basset. The Latin inscription incised around the tomb records the death of Basset on 13 December 1423 and prays God to have mercy on his soul.

In 1536 the priory at Ewenny was among the religious foundations dissolved as part of Henry VIII's reforms, and the emotions of communities throughout the Vale, including St Hilary, must have been stirred at this news. But it was with the accession of Edward VI in 1547 that ever more radical assaults on the old familiar liturgy and doctrine were made. Images were removed and destroyed, paintings defaced, and in 1553 St Hilary was among the Vale churches robbed of ornaments and vestments by Royal Commissioners, one of whom was William Basset of Beaupre. What trauma must have been experienced by priest and parishioners as they watched treasured possessions removed from their church—a cope of green silk, chasubles of velvet, taffeta, satin and fustian, crosses including one of copper gilt, a holy water pot and more than twenty candlesticks. Little of real value would have been left in the church, just a few items allowed as necessary for parish worship, and for those who witnessed the despoliation of their church the experience must have been traumatic. After the departure of the Commissioners, priest and congregation returned to a strangely bare and austere building. With the accession of the catholic Queen Mary hopes were raised of the return of church property, and when in 1555/6 the then priest at St Hilary, David Llewelyn, compiled a list of the goods removed from his church he must have entertained the hope that restitution would be made. It never was.

But amidst such disruption and change there were reassuring expressions of continuity. Many laymen had profited from the dispersal of church property but were concerned enough for their immortal souls to continue to make pious benefactions to the church, and in 1559 St Hilary church benefited to the sum of 40 shillings from the Will of Sir Rice Mansel of Oxwich, the man who had purchased the buildings and lands of the dissolved abbey of Margam and who, through his first marriage to Eleanor Basset of Beaupre, enjoyed a life interest in the old mansion house on the banks of the Thaw.

For many parishioners, both English and Welsh speaking, the introduction of a new English liturgy was confusing and bewildering, and it seems clear that affection for the old, familiar, albeit little understood, latin forms of service and prayer lingered long and that some clung tenaciously to the old religion of Rome. One priest who found himself out of sympathy with the Elizabethan religious settlement was John Lingo. Formerly a monk at Llantarnum (co. Mon.), and later chantry priest at Cowbridge, Lingo was appointed vicar of St Hilary in the late 1550s. Already in 1560 he was non resident, by 1563 he was described as 'not Resydent upon his vicarage nor knowen where he is at this present', and undoubtedly his adherence to the old faith had caused him to abandon his parish. His flock, tied to their community, had little option but to accept change and conform.

THE MANOR OF ST HILARY

At the end of the eleventh century (*c.*1093) the Norman baron Robert Fitzhamon and his followers swept into South Wales and began their conquest of the old Welsh kingdom of Morgannwg. From his stronghold in Cardiff, Fitzhamon moved westwards, subduing, settling and reorganising the lowland areas of the Vale of Glamorgan before penetrating further west and north. In these fertile lowlands the Anglo-Normans built castles and churches, and established manorial economies whereby the land was farmed, for the benefit of the lord of the manor, by tenants living in close communities, usually under the protective shadow of castle or fortified manor house.

Sometime in the twelfth century St Hilary manor was created within the lordship of Llanblethian/Talyfan. The earliest identified lords of Llanblethian are members of the St Quentin family, but so scant is the documentary evidence for this period that both the activities of the St Quentins and the history of the manor of St Hilary remain clouded in obscurity. What can be said in this context with reasonable certainty is that the first lord of the manor of St Hilary was a member of the de Cardiff family.

The de Cardiffs entered Glamorgan with, or in the immediate wake of, Fitzhamon, establishing their first territorial base at Llantrithyd where a twelfth-century castle ringwork has been identified. Precisely how or when they acquired the manor of St Hilary is not known, although the suggestion has been made that the de Cardiffs were associated with the St Quentins when that family established its authority in Llanblethian and were rewarded for their services with the grant of St Hilary. When Richard de Cardiff died in 1197 the manor or ½ knight's fee of St Hilary was listed among his possessions. Sometime in the next century the Bassets succeeded the de Cardiffs as lords of the manor of St Hilary, Elias Basset being recorded as holding the ½ knight's fee, valued at £10 in 1262.

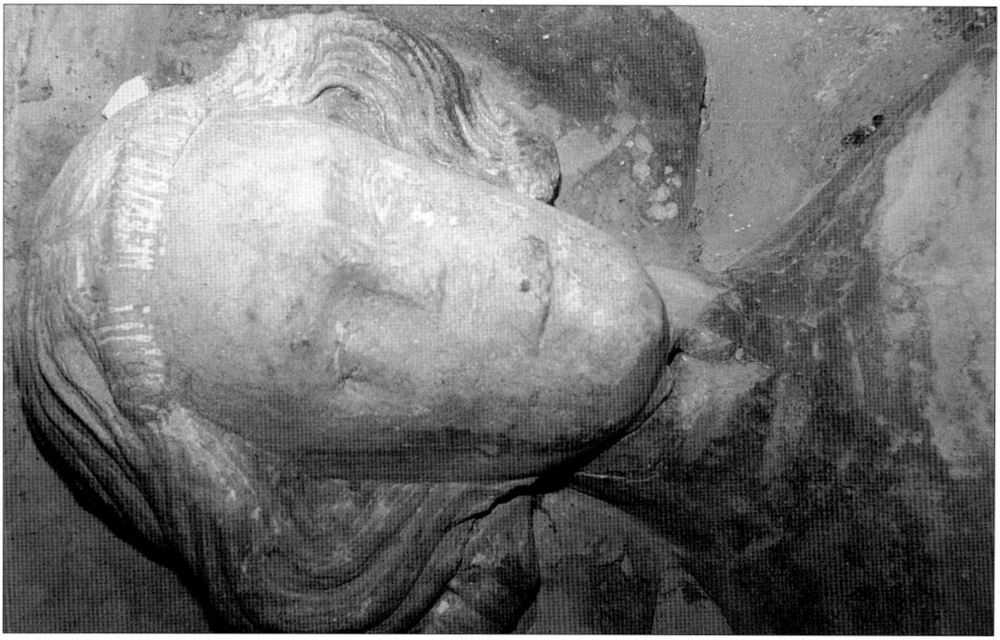

7. Youthful features of the civilian believed to be a member of the de Cardiff family, lords of the manor of St Hilary in C13th.

Again it is unclear how the Bassets acquired the manor, although it is generally assumed that it was through marriage with a de Cardiff heiress.

In 1245 the lordship of Llanblethian passed into the hands of Richard de Clare, chief lord of Glamorgan, and henceforth the manor of St Hilary was held directly of de Clare and his successors—Despensers, Beauchamps, Nevilles and, in the fifteenth century, the Crown. In 1317 it was among the de Clare lands ordered to be delivered to Hugh le Despenser, and in 1440, when listed among the possessions of Isabella Countess of Warwick, it was described as 'formerly held by Thomas Basset'.

The status of St Hilary as a manor is certain, but where was the early focus of that manor? The de Cardiffs would have had a base from which they and their stewards exercised the rights of lordship, rights which included the holding of manorial courts to regulate manorial tenancies, exact manorial dues and services, and enforce manorial customs. Strategically and economically St Hilary was a significant territorial asset in the hands of its first Anglo-Norman lords who must have erected some form of building here to stand as a symbol of their authority. But to date no trace of such a structure has been discovered, no twelfth-century castle even on the diminutive scale of nearby Llanquian, no fortified manor house earlier than the fourteenth century. It is the Bassets, not the de Cardiffs, who appear to have left the earliest surviving architectural evidence of the Anglo-Norman presence in St Hilary.

The name of Basset, which endured for many centuries in St Hilary, has long overshadowed that of de Cardiff. In some genealogical compilations claims have been made that members of the Basset family accompanied Fitzhamon into Glamorgan and were rewarded for their services with the grant of the lordship of St Hilary. Such claims must be regarded as bogus, but they have tended to further obscure the early history of St Hilary and of the de Cardiff family. Only the recumbent effigy of the young layman in the church provides a tangible link with the first lords of the manor of St Hilary, for the effigy is believed to be that of a member of the de Cardiff family. And it is interesting to note that

8. Detail from the de Cardiff effigy showing the long gauntlets clasped in the hand.

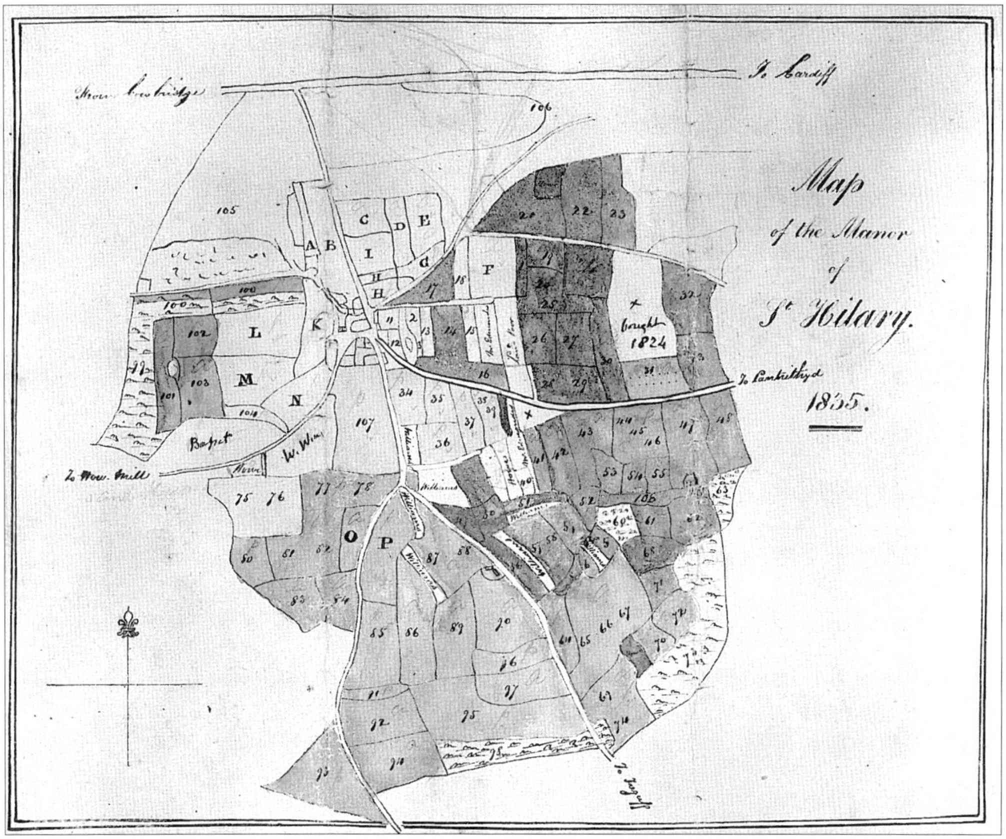

9. Map of St Hilary manor, 1835.

the youth, clothed in a long, plain tunic and wearing ankle-high shoes, holds in his hand a pair of gauntlets. These long gloves may, perhaps, be symbolic of the annual payment of a sparrowhawk said to be due from the de Cardiffs to their overlord.

With the appearance of the Bassets in St Hilary, and their identification with Beaupre, a more complete picture of ownership and descent begins to appear. What remains unclear is whether the names of St Hilary and Beaupre were used interchangeably to describe one manorial entity or whether there were in fact two distinct manors. A statement in a survey of Llanblethian, dated 1630, declares that William Basset held 'his manor of Beaupire under the said lordship of knight's service, and ought to pay yearly a sparrowhawk', but the general consensus of scholarly opinion has long been that Beaupre was neither a manor in its own right nor a sub manor of St Hilary and that the two names were used interchangeably. However, seventeenth and eighteenth century conveyances cloud the issue by referring quite specifically to the manors of St Hilary and Beaupre and assigning particular lands to each, while in the nineteenth century antiquarians hedged their bets by writing that within the manor of St Hilary was 'the manor or reputed manor of Beaupre'.

A map of St Hilary manor drawn up in 1835 for the then lord of the manor, the Reverend John Montgomery Traherne, excludes Beaupre lands from its boundaries, and while some nineteenth-century writers accorded the title lord of the manor of Beaupre to a member of the Basset family then in possession of the Beaupre estate there does not appear to be any documentary evidence for this title. Certainly when the Beaupre estate was put up for sale at the beginning of the twentieth century no reference was made to manorial rights or titles.

Rooted in the medieval past, the manor of St Hilary survived well into the nineteenth century, its customs and institutions an integral if increasingly less significant part of local life. Its foundation, early history and evolution still pose many unanswered questions. One link with St Hilary's manorial past does, however, survive as an identifiable feature of the landscape above and to the north of the village. Here, surrounded on two sides by the wider expanse of common land called Stalling Down, is the surviving remnant of St Hilary Down, formerly the common of the manor of St Hilary where tenants had communal grazing and other rights, a tract of open land that was an important part of the manorial economy.

10. Stone marking the western boundary of St Hilary manor, erected by J. M. Traherne, 1845.

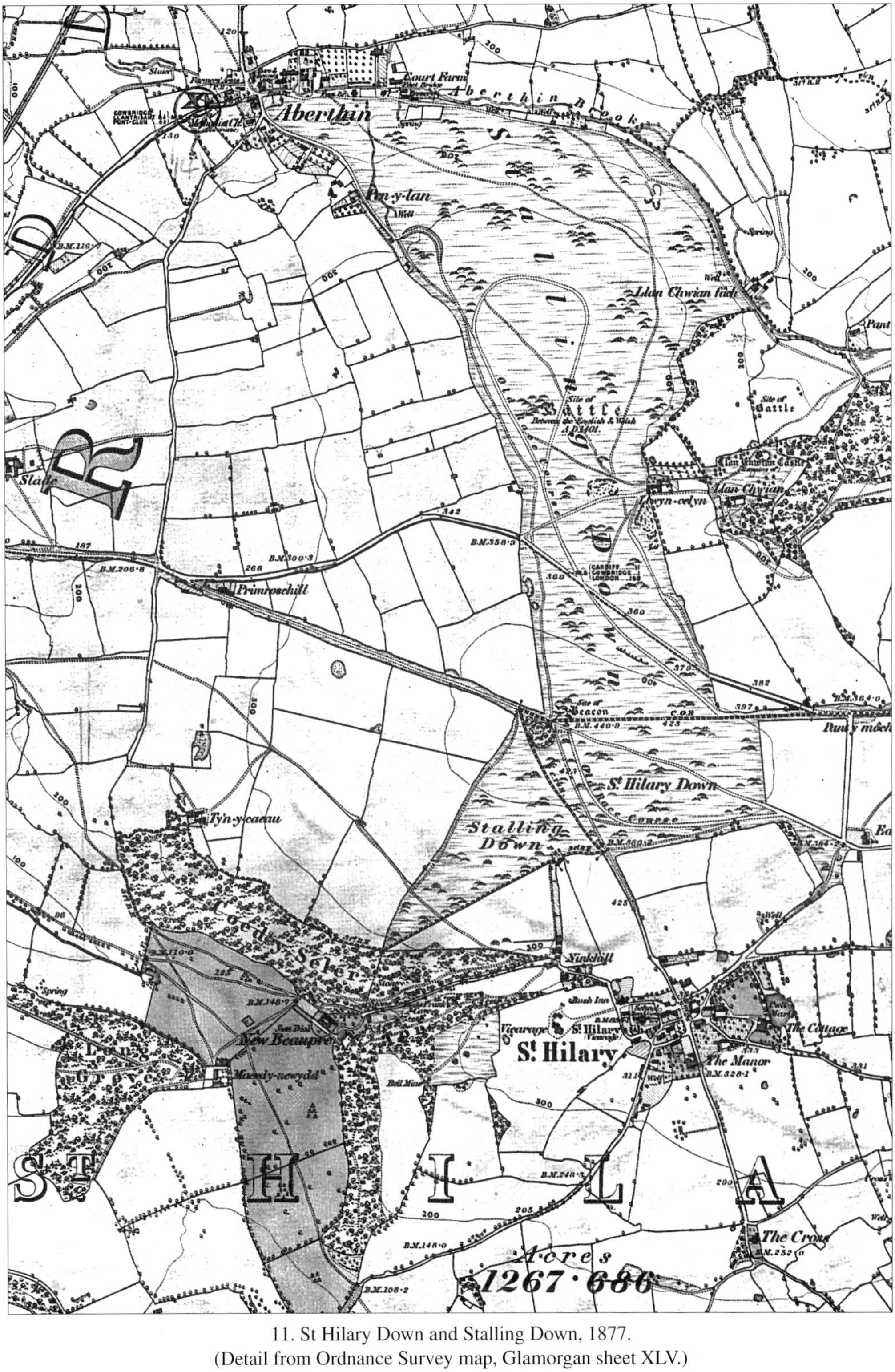

11. St Hilary Down and Stalling Down, 1877.
(Detail from Ordnance Survey map, Glamorgan sheet XLV.)

THE BASSETS OF BEAUPRE

The name Beaupre is clearly Anglo-Norman in origin and can be assumed to have been introduced into the locality by the de Cardiffs or the Bassets. Derived from the old French *beau repaire* (beautiful retreat) the name is unusual in this area but has numerous parallels in England, for example Beaurepaire and Beaulieu in Hampshire, and Belvoir in Leicestershire. Locally the name is known by its Welsh form *Bewpyr* (pronounced Bewper).

The name first appears in a document dated 1376 when a John Basset is described as 'of St Hilary and Bewerpere'. Thereafter the names of Basset and Beaupre are inextricably linked, but as the earliest identifiable fabric within Old Beaupre house dates from *c.*1300 it is impossible to say whether the de Cardiffs or the Bassets were the first builders on this favoured site close to the river Thaw.

Claims have been made that long before either of these families made their presence felt in the Vale of Glamorgan the site was named *maes essyllt* (fair meadow) and that it was home to the Welsh family of Syssylt, forebears of the mighty Cecils. Furthermore, the fact that the name of Basset was prominent in the ranks of the English nobility and gentry in the twelfth and thirteenth centuries prompted some inventive minds of later centuries to ignore the lack of evidence linking English Bassets with their Glamorgan namesakes, and to accord to Beaupre the honour of hosting the assembly of barons who drafted Magna Carta (1215). Legend is always an integral and intriguing strand in the history of places and people, and the lure of these stories is still strong, but they have no validated place in the history of Beaupre.

The earliest house to be identified at Beaupre, and of which few traces remain, stood south of the main range of buildings that now survive. Entered through a medieval gatehouse, it appears to have comprised an open courtyard surrounded by domestic buildings. Whether first occupied by the de Cardiffs or the Bassets, the house owed its remodelling and rebuilding from the fourteenth century onwards to the Basset family, and it was the Bassets who were responsible for the major building works carried out in the sixteenth century.

From the Thomas Basset whose effigy in the church depicts him in full plate armour and whose death is recorded in 1423, Beaupre passed in almost unbroken line of

12. Old Beaupre (photographed 1998).

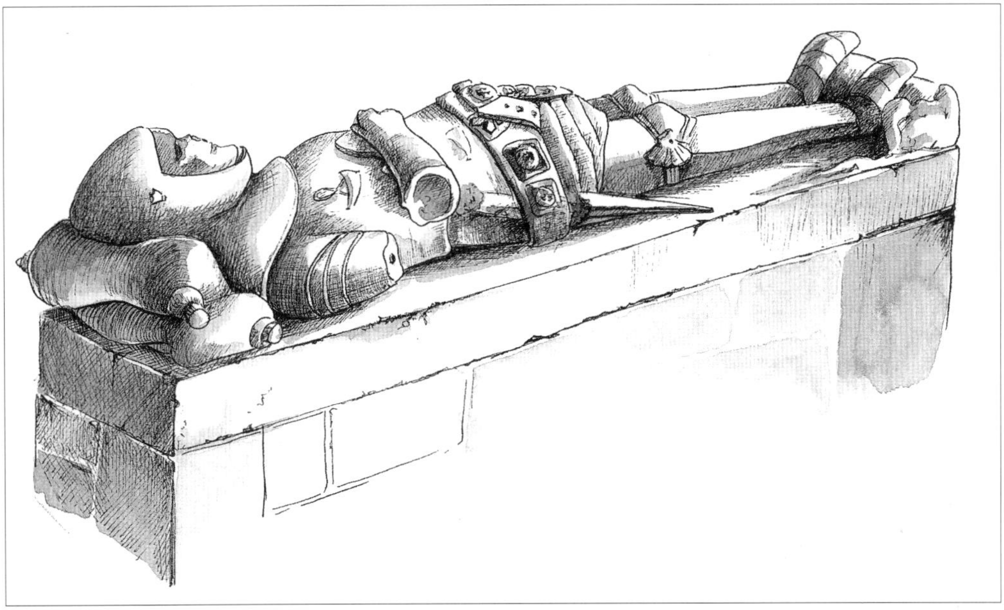

13. Thomas Basset (d. 1423).

succession from father to son until the eighteenth century, with each generation residing at the old family mansion. Only with the death of James Basset *c.*1502 did the Basset succession falter, for James had no sons, just one daughter, Eleanor, a minor at the time of her father's death. Eleanor's arranged marriage to the young Rice Mansel of Oxwich in 1511 was short-lived and childless, ending with Eleanor's death sometime before 1520, but her husband, Sir Rice Mansel as he became in 1527, retained a life interest in Beaupre, remarried, and by the second of his three wives fathered a daughter, Catherine. Before his death in 1559 Sir Rice saw Catherine married to her cousin William Basset (sheriff 1558), the reversionary heir to the Beaupre estate, and by that marriage Basset ownership of the property was firmly re-established.

Rebuilding and extension of the old house, probably begun during the occupancy of Sir Rice Mansel, was continued by his Basset successors, and the scale and nature of that rebuilding gives some indication of the wealth and status of the Basset family in the sixteenth century. Beaupre, idyllically sited, impressively large and suitably fashionable with its blend of Elizabethan and medieval features, epitomised affluence and emphasised the prominence of the Bassets in Glamorgan society.

The rebuilding included the construction of the outer gatehouse with its decorated porch in 1586, and culminated in the erection of the magnificent inner porch in 1600. Incorporating the three orders of classical architecture (Doric, Ionic and Corinthian), embellished with an heraldic achievement on which was carved the Basset arms (3 bugle horns stringed) and motto (*gwell angau na chwilydd*—rather death than dishonour), and with inscribed panels declaring that 'Richarde Bassett . . . bwylt this porche . . . Ano.1600', the inner porch is a remarkable architectural feature, as impressive today in its ruinous setting as it must have been in the heyday of the house.

Here again 'tradition' from the pen of Iolo Morganwg colours historical fact, for according to Iolo the porch was the work of Richard Twrch, a stonemason who, with his

14. Effigy of Sir Rice Mansel of Oxwich and Beaupre (d. 1559) in Margam Abbey church. (CADW. Welsh Historic Monuments. Crown Copyright.)

brother William, worked the Sutton quarries near Bridgend. Sibling rivalry and unrequited love led Richard to leave the county to work first in London and later in Italy, from where he returned to demonstrate his considerable talents as artist and sculptor. Such were those skills that they won him commissions from some of the county's leading gentry, among them Sir Richard Basset of Beaupre. 'Of what authenticity these traditions are must be left to judgements greatly superior to mine' wrote Iolo, himself a stonemason by trade. What no one can question is the superb craftsmanship of the Beaupre porch.

In addition to their Beaupre property the Bassets also had estates in England, including property in Gloucestershire and Somerset, and it was at Monkton Combe church near Bath that William Basset was buried in 1586 at the age of eighty. A splendid monument was

15. The inner porch at Old Beaupre, built 1600.
(CADW. Welsh Historic Monuments. Crown Copyright.)

erected in the church to commemorate him and his wife Catherine (née Mansel) who died in 1593 also aged eighty.

When absent from Beaupre the Bassets depended upon stewards and others to manage their estate. In 1573 William Basset appointed Roger Seys of 'Bolston' [Bonvilston] as his steward in the lordships and manors of St Hilary, Treguff, Llantrithyd and Penon. And it may well have been Seys who oversaw the laying-out of formal gardens in the meadow land between house and river, traces of which can still be discerned today, and the creation (or restoration) of fishponds in the valley, schemes recognised as the work of William Basset. When in residence the family could worship in their private chapel, the chapel of

16. Old Beaupre in its heyday. A restored view showing the probable appearance of the house. (Crown Copyright: Royal Commission on the Ancient and Historical Monuments of Wales.)

St Mary of Beaupre, first recorded in the sixteenth century but possibly of medieval origin. It is not known if the chapel was located within the house or was a detached building.

Iolo Morganwg's claim that a great gorsedd of bards was held at Beaupre in 1681 is probably wildly exaggerated, but what is certain is that the Bassets of Beaupre had long been patrons of the Welsh bards. Rhisiart Morgannwg (*fl.*1480s and 1490s), one of a celebrated circle of bards from Tir Iarll (Llangynwyd) is known to have visited Beaupre, and Meurug Dafydd (*fl.*1560s-1590s), a noted professional bard, sang to the Bassets on several occasions. For one panegyric addressed to his patron, William Basset, Meurig was rewarded with a 'noble' [6s. 8d.]; but another of his compositions was less favourably received and was consigned to the fire by Basset. The Bassets' patronage of the bards continued well into the seventeenth century, and the Margam bard, Edward Dafydd (*c.*1600-78), in praising Sir Richard Basset, graced him with the lavish title *Eryr y Bewpyr euriad*. Strictly translated as the eagle of gilded Beaupre, the phrase may well have been interpreted as bestowing the accolade 'golden eagle' upon the patron.

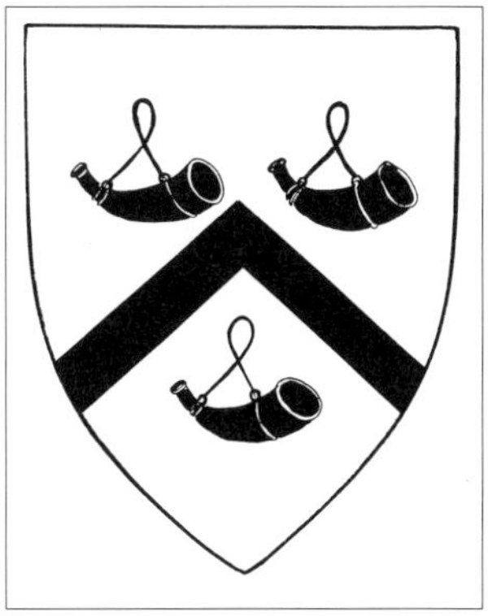

17. The Basset family coat of arms (three bugle horns stringed).

During the sixteenth and the early-seventeenth century members of the Basset family, as befitted their status, took a prominent role in the official life of the county. William Basset served as sheriff in 1544, his son William in 1558, and his grandson Richard in 1597 and 1609. Later generations continued this tradition—William Basset in 1622 and Richard Basset in 1643.

Shrieval power, particularly in the turbulent sixteenth century, was considerable and open to abuse, and several of Glamorgan's sixteenth-century sheriffs appeared before the courts to answer charges of abusing their position while in office. No Basset seems to have been brought before the courts while serving as sheriff, but the involvement of the owners of Beaupre in local feuds and rivalries did, on occasion, bring them into conflict not only with their neighbours but also with the law.

In May 1537 William Carne of Cowbridge was waylaid and attacked by three of Sir Rice Mansel's servants in Cowbridge, and although Mansel denied knowledge of the assault he was accused by Carne not only of a blatant breach of the peace but also of attempting to pervert the course of justice by intimidating local court officials, notably one Roger Carne. Carne and Mansel took their grievances to the Court of Star Chamber in London where Mansel vigorously rebutted the charges against him. According to his version of events, he had ridden peaceably into Cowbridge to attend the court with no intention of causing 'hurt or displeasure' to William Carne. He did admit that he and a number of his servants were dressed in armour and carried bows and arrows, javelins and crossbows, but said that this was a necessary precaution because of threats from Carne and his servants.

A more serious affray took place in Cowbridge in June 1576 involving followers of the Bassets of Beaupre and the Turbervilles of Penllyn. Swords were drawn, and the brawl 'a great disquiet to the whole country' again resulted in legal proceedings in the Court of Star Chamber. And in 1608 John Stradling, sheriff of Glamorgan, brought a case in the same court against William Basset of Beaupre and his son for 'rescuing' Price Williams of Broughton from arrest for debt at Llantwit Major. Such incidents provide graphic insights into the arrogant abuse of power by local gentry, into local rivalries and jealousies and into the volatile society of the period.

At the beginning of the seventeenth century the Bassets of Beaupre, resident in their splendidly refurbished mansion, were among Glamorgan's wealthiest gentry families with an annual income estimated at over £1000. By the end of the Civil War they were in serious financial difficulties; by the end of the century they were all but ruined, and undoubtedly their prominent role in support of the royalist cause was a major factor in stripping them of wealth and power.

In 1643, Richard Basset, sheriff of Glamorgan, headed the Glamorgan contingent besieging the parliamentary-held city of Gloucester, and was knighted for his services to the king. Two years later he served, briefly, as governor of Cardiff Castle, but having been

18. The outer gatehouse at Old Beaupre.
(CADW. Welsh Historic Monuments. Crown Copyright.)

19. Artist's impression of the Battle of St Fagans, 8 May 1648.
(Reproduced from an original watercolour by Karel M. Toman, by kind permission of Raymond Bowen.)

ignominiously ousted from that position, led a royalist contingent to Hereford where he was captured when the city fell to the parliamentarians. In 1648 he was one of the leading royalist rebels in Glamorgan who took up arms in a doomed attempt to reverse the parliamentary victory of 1646, and as a 'delinquent' Sir Richard Basset was heavily fined by parliament—he had to pay £753. Political exigencies probably led to him spending several years abroad. Financial pressures must have been a prime cause of his abandonment of Beaupre 'his chief dwelling-house and very goodly and fair demesnes thereunto belonging' in favour of the more modest dwelling at nearby Fishweir, a property acquired by the marriage of his great-grandfather with the heiress Catherine Bowen.

Economically, politically and socially, the impact of the Civil War and its aftermath on the Bassets of Beaupre was crippling. The impact upon the wider community of St Hilary is harder to gauge. The Bassets, unswervingly loyal to their king, would have expected, indeed demanded, equal loyalty from their tenants and servants, and once the conflict began in the summer of 1642 landlord and tenants alike became embroiled in the great affairs of state. Some tenants would have ridden off with Sir Richard Basset and experienced conflict at first hand. Others, who stayed at home, must have seen and heard horses and men, parliamentarian and royalist, marching across Stalling Down during the progress of the war. In 1647 Sir Richard, with other prominent royalists including Sir Edward Thomas of Llanmihangel, mustered royalist supporters in Cowbridge, and if reports of 1000 men converging on the town are to be believed, this must have provided an impressive spectacle.

Not until the end of the Civil War was a battle fought in Glamorgan, but in May 1648 the bloody battle of St Fagans ended in the heavy defeat of the royalists and in the

20. Detail from the Basset tomb showing the mutilation of the effigy.

21. The inner courtyard at Old Beaupre.
(CADW. Welsh Historic Monuments. Crown copyright.)

slaughter and capture of many of their men. Fleeing royalists were pursued across the Vale by the victorious parliamentarians, and St Hilary with its associations with the defiant Bassets may well have been a particular target of parliamentary vengeance. To this day, mutilation of the Basset effigy in the church is attributed to Cromwell's soldiers.

Sir Richard Basset, who had seen his king executed and the royalist cause destroyed, lived long enough to see the monarchy restored. He was buried in St Hilary church on 24th February 1664, leaving an inheritance much diminished by his involvement in the Civil War. During the lifetime of his sons the family fortunes, far from being restored, were further undermined, and the Bassets of Beaupre headed, inexorably, towards financial ruin.

Sir Richard's eldest son, William, who was buried in Westminster Abbey in 1667, is said to have squandered his already depleted inheritance by an extravagant lifestyle in London. Richard, the second son, stood surety, with others, for Sir Edward Stradling of St Donats, in the vast sum of £21,000. When Stradling defaulted on the Bond the Bassets of Beaupre were, effectively, ruined.

In his Will, dated 26th December 1691, that second son, now styled 'Sir Richard Basset of Beaupre' specified that his property at 'Glasonbury' (co. Somerset) was to be sold to pay off his debts. His St Hilary/Beaupre estate, subject to provisions for his widow Priscilla, his four daughters and a younger son, descended to his eldest son Philip Basset. But by this date the family's debts were overwhelming and the burden on the Beaupre estate of raising a £1500 marriage portion for Jane Basset, the eldest daughter, and £1000 for each of her younger siblings, stretched resources to breaking point. Early in the next century Philip Basset and his mother, the widowed Dame Priscilla, entered into an Agreement with a Christopher Brewster, gentleman, for the sale of the family estate in St Hilary and Llanblethian. The long association of the Bassets with Beaupre was broken but not, as it turned out, permanently, for in the nineteenth century the Bassets would be reinstated as owners.

VILLAGE AND PARISH IN THE SIXTEENTH AND SEVENTEENTH CENTURIES

While the major land-owning families and their activities can be traced, albeit incompletely, from the medieval period onwards, members of the wider community of St Hilary are rarely identifiable before the eighteenth century.

Alongside the name of the Reverend David Llewelyn, vicar of St Hilary in 1555/6, are those of two parishioners—Thomas ap Morgan Harrye and William Thomas Dyo, almost certainly the then churchwarden and one of his predecessors. And two long-serving priests can be identified with St Hilary in the seventeenth century, the Reverend Rowland Williams who died in office in 1682 after serving as vicar for a remarkable sixty-eight years, and his successor the Reverend Joseph Merrick who was vicar from 1682-1723.

Among the small number of laymen who emerge from obscurity is William ap John of St Hilary, yeoman. In 1522 he was in possession of part of the manor of Eglwysbrewis. Later conveyances of the property reveal that William was the father of Thomas William and grandfather of Edward William who, by the 1570s, was styling himself 'gentleman'—one of the earliest known examples of 'social advancement' in St Hilary! An example of mobility of a different sort is provided a century later by the Roger family. When, in October 1666, Edward Roger, tailor, leased a messuage and land in Llantrithyd he and his wife Mary and son George moved out of St Hilary and into the adjoining parish.

Robert Williams of St Hilary, who died in 1661, was a gentleman of substance and member of a family associated also with Aberthin. Among numerous charitable bequests specified in his Will, written in 1658 after the death of his only son, were two for the benefit of St Hilary—10s. 0d. towards the 'reparaton' of the parish church, and an annuity of 8s. 0d. charged on 'lands called the Lake' for the poor of the parish, to be distributed monthly in bread to those most in need.

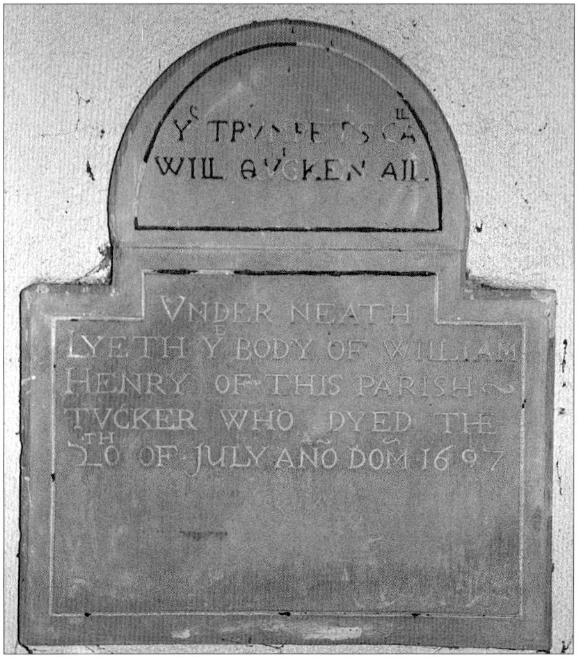

22. Memorial in the church to William Henry of St Hilary, Tucker (d. 1697), with the text 'The trumpets call will quicken all'

Such charitable bequests are unexceptional, but the money for the repair of the church may have been particularly welcome. Puritan zeal during the years of the Interregnum had sought to obliterate all traces, real or imagined, of a 'catholic' past from places of worship, and further despoliation during those years had left many a parish church greatly impoverished.

In his Will Robert Williams made due provision for his widow, Catherine. To enable her to live in comfort for the remainder of her life certain properties, including messuages and lands in St Hilary, were reserved for her enjoyment

23. Hearth in the great chamber at Old Beaupre (photographed 1998).

and she was to have the use of 'all houshould stuffe' in the family house in St Hilary. She was also given 'six kyne, forty sheepe, two twelve-month old beasts and two two-yeare old beasts' and the choice of her late husband's horses or £5 in lieu thereof.

Such glimpses of individual family circumstances are rare. A broader view of St Hilary's inhabitants in the seventeenth century is provided by the Hearth Tax Returns of 1670 which list every householder in the parish together with the number of taxable hearths in each property, and while it is difficult to link any other than the great landowners with a particular property, and impossible to determine exactly how many individuals were living in each household, the Returns do provide valuable insights into the population. A total of thirty-one hearth tax payers are listed for St Hilary, together with an additional seven individuals described as too poor to pay the tax. Lady Martha Basset of Beaupre heads the list, liable for payment on the ten hearths in her residence. Next in the hierarchy comes Katherine Morgan (5 hearths), Evan Thomas (4 hearths) and Edd. Lewis (3 hearths), all the remaining householders being assessed on two or a single hearth.

The house or cottage occupied by William Thomas had two hearths, but where in the village it stood we do not know. However, William Thomas was undoubtedly the parish constable whose name appears, in his official capacity, at the end of the Return.

Some of the houses in which the families listed in the Return lived are still standing. It is tempting to place Evan Thomas in Village Farm where four hearths of sixteenth-century date can still be seen. And might the property now called The Old Post Office have been home to the Jenkin Bassett who, in 1670, was assessed on two hearths one of which was described as 'unfinished', for the surviving mid-seventeenth-century fabric here displays clear evidence of two stages of building. And Katherine Morgan with her five hearths may have lived at the Great House (alias The Manor House) in 1670, but so drastically was this

24. Village farm, a mid-C16th hearth-passage house. A cutaway drawing showing the main features of the house. (Crown Copyright: Royal Commission on the Ancient and Historical Monuments of Wales.)

25. The Bush inn, *c*.1913.

house altered *c.*1800 that its earlier form cannot be determined. The Bush Inn would have been among the single hearth properties listed and, although radically altered in succeeding centuries, the old inn still retains its massive hearth and the essential features of a mid-sixteenth-century hearth-passage house.

A list of the names of families resident in St Hilary at the end of the seventeenth century includes those of William(s), John, Rosser, Lewis, Scacy, Evan, Prichard, How(e) and David. The total population of the parish at this date was probably no more than 150, and many families would have spoken Welsh as their mother tongue. Few individuals would have received any formal education, but in 1675 there is evidence that a small school was being conducted for poor children in St Hilary under the auspices of a charitable trust. The Welsh Trust was the first charity to establish schools in Glamorgan, and the St Hilary school with its ten pupils (in 1678) was the smallest in the county. Such schools were usually administered by the vicar and churchwardens, and instruction was in English, but the Trust also disseminated literature in Welsh, including copies of the Welsh translation of the Bible, and may have provided such a volume in St Hilary. The school does not appear to have continued beyond a few years, and not until the 1760s with the appearance of Circulating Schools would 'education' be provided again in the village. Nothing is known of the children who attended the Welsh Trust school, virtually nothing is known about their families and neighbours. Only in the next century does the community suddenly come alive, when, in the pages of the St Hilary parish registers and other records, the lives of 'ordinary' people are brought into sharp focus.

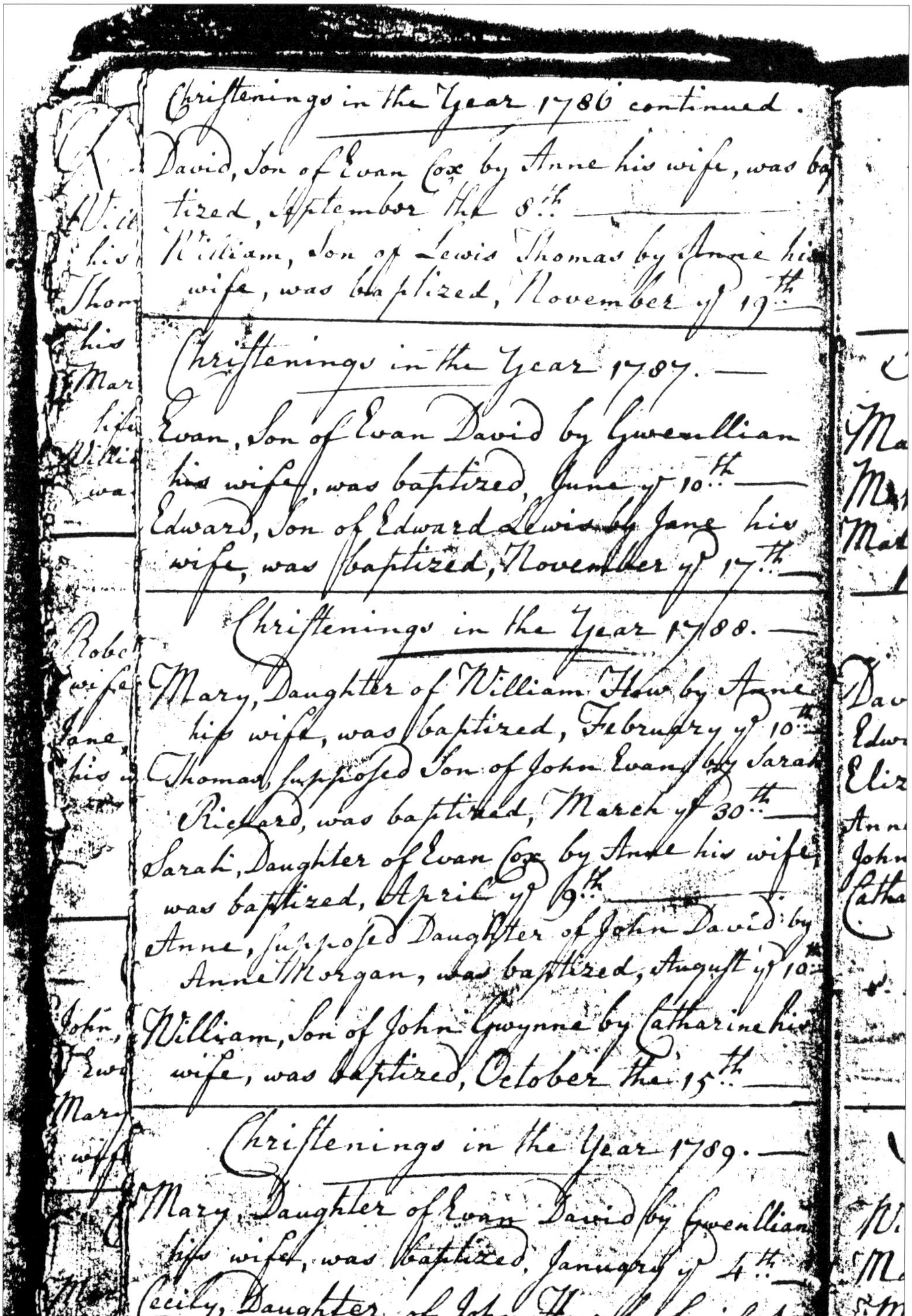

Christenings in the Year 1786 continued.

David, Son of Evan Cox by Anne his wife, was baptized, September the 8th

William, Son of Lewis Thomas by Anne his wife, was baptized, November ye 19th

Christenings in the Year 1787.

Evan, Son of Evan David by Gwenllian his wife, was baptized, June ye 10th

Edward, Son of Edward Lewis by Jane his wife, was baptized, November ye 17th

Christenings in the Year 1788.

Mary, Daughter of William How by Anne his wife, was baptized, February ye 10th

Thomas, supposed Son of John Evans by Sarah Richard, was baptized, March ye 30th

Sarah, Daughter of Evan Cox by Anne his wife was baptized, April ye 6th

Anne, supposed Daughter of John David by Anne Morgan, was baptized, August ye 10th

William, Son of John Gwynne by Catharine his wife, was baptized, October the 15th

Christenings in the Year 1789.

Mary, Daughter of Evan David by Gwenllian his wife, was baptized, January ye 4th

Cecily, Daughter of John How by Cecily his

26. Entries in the parish register: Christenings, 1786-89.
(Glamorgan Record Office.)

VILLAGE AND PARISH IN THE EIGHTEENTH CENTURY

Life and Death

Among the first entries in the St Hilary parish registers are the marriage of Thomas Lougher of St Hilary and Anne David of Cowbridge in June 1690, the baptism of Barbara the daughter of William Hopkin a month earlier, and the burial of Richard the son of David Powel in June the same year. Unsurprisingly, the name of Basset figures prominently among the early entries—Richard Basset baptised in November 1690, his father Sir Richard buried in January 1692 and a succession of Basset baptisms, marriages and burials in the early years of the next century.

Joy and tragedy were close companions for most families. The baptism of Elizabeth, daughter of a Thomas Bassett senior, in May 1715 was followed swiftly by her burial a month later, a sequence of events familiar to many parents. The Holland family's story is not untypical. In September 1709 Nicholas and Roger the infant sons of Rees Holland were baptised in St Hilary church. A month later two other Holland children, Roger and Elizabeth, were buried, and in July 1711 young Nicholas followed them to the grave. In June 1716 Prudence Holland, the children's mother, died, probably in childbirth, leaving her husband with several children, the youngest of whom was just four years old when he and his surviving siblings were orphaned in 1720.

Infant mortality dominates many pages of the registers. Only three burials were recorded in St Hilary in 1792, but all were children—Margaret Thomas aged one year and nine months, Catherine Thomas aged two and William Jones aged eleven.

Alongside the sagas of infant mortality and orphaned children the parish registers also reveal that some parishioners lived to a ripe old age. Two members of the Lougher family, Robert and Thomas both died in 1784, Robert aged eighty-two and Thomas aged eighty-six. Philip Cadogan enjoyed eighty-nine years of life from 1717-1806. Anne Edward (d.1786) aged eighty-six and Alice Lovat (d.1791) aged seventy-one were among the oldest female inhabitants of the parish.

Entries in the registers also divulge the occupations of some parishioners. Thomas David the carrier, of Howe Mill, was buried in 1699. In the first half of the eighteenth century the names of Rees William miller, Morgan Jones glover, John Lewis tailor, William Hopkin weaver, and Edward Williams and Edward Lewis millers appear among the entries. And in the 1750s there is a glimpse of small-scale industrial activity in the parish when John Watkins and Richard Jenkins are described as miners [i.e. lead miners].

Occasionally the bare entries in the registers are supplemented by other contemporary records. The register notes the burial of a Morgan Thomas aged sixty-five on 16 October 1791. The diarist William Thomas of Michaelston-super-Ely imparts the information that the deceased was the son of Gibbon Thomas of Goldsland in Wenvoe, and of Beaupre, and that having once been 'a great farmer at Beaupre' he had 'since reduced in the world' and become a schoolmaster at St Nicholas. William Thomas lost no opportunity to lay bare the misfortunes of families and individuals, and from another diary entry we learn that the David Williams of Cowbridge East Village, who was buried at St Hilary in January 1790, had once been 'a great malster' but had ended his days as clerk of Cowbridge Hundred. A glimpse into the domestic circumstances of the widow Mary Thomas, who died in June

27. Churchyard headstone commemorating Evan John (d. 1743 aged 26) and his wife Anne (d. 1761 aged 59).

1714 and was buried in the churchyard, is provided by the valuation of her personal estate drawn up soon after her death. Her worldly goods were few, just a bed, a chair, a small brass pan and an iron crock, and these together with her wearing apparel and linen were valued at a mere £3 10s. 0d. But even a feather bed and a chair denote a level of comfort denied to many of St Hilary's inhabitants at that date, and Mary Thomas also had a nest egg of £100 put out 'at interest' to provide her with a small income.

Most of the burial entries relate to individuals whose families were resident in St Hilary, but occasionally itinerants found an untimely resting place in the parish. Gwenllian, daughter of Rowland the tinker, was buried in June 1698; Elizabeth a poor vagrant was buried in the depths of winter 1701/2.

The latter's burial would have been paid for by the parish from a parish rate levied on the more prosperous inhabitants and administered by the locally appointed officials. From the sixteenth century to the nineteenth century each parish was very much an autonomous unit, responsible for regulating its own affairs through its own officials, notably the overseers of the poor, the churchwardens and the 'petty' or parish constables. And in the accounts compiled by these officials in the performance of their duties are recorded the regular preoccupations and exceptional events of parish and village life. The detailed accounts for St Hilary, covering the best part of a century (1728-1821) provide rich cameos of events and personalities.

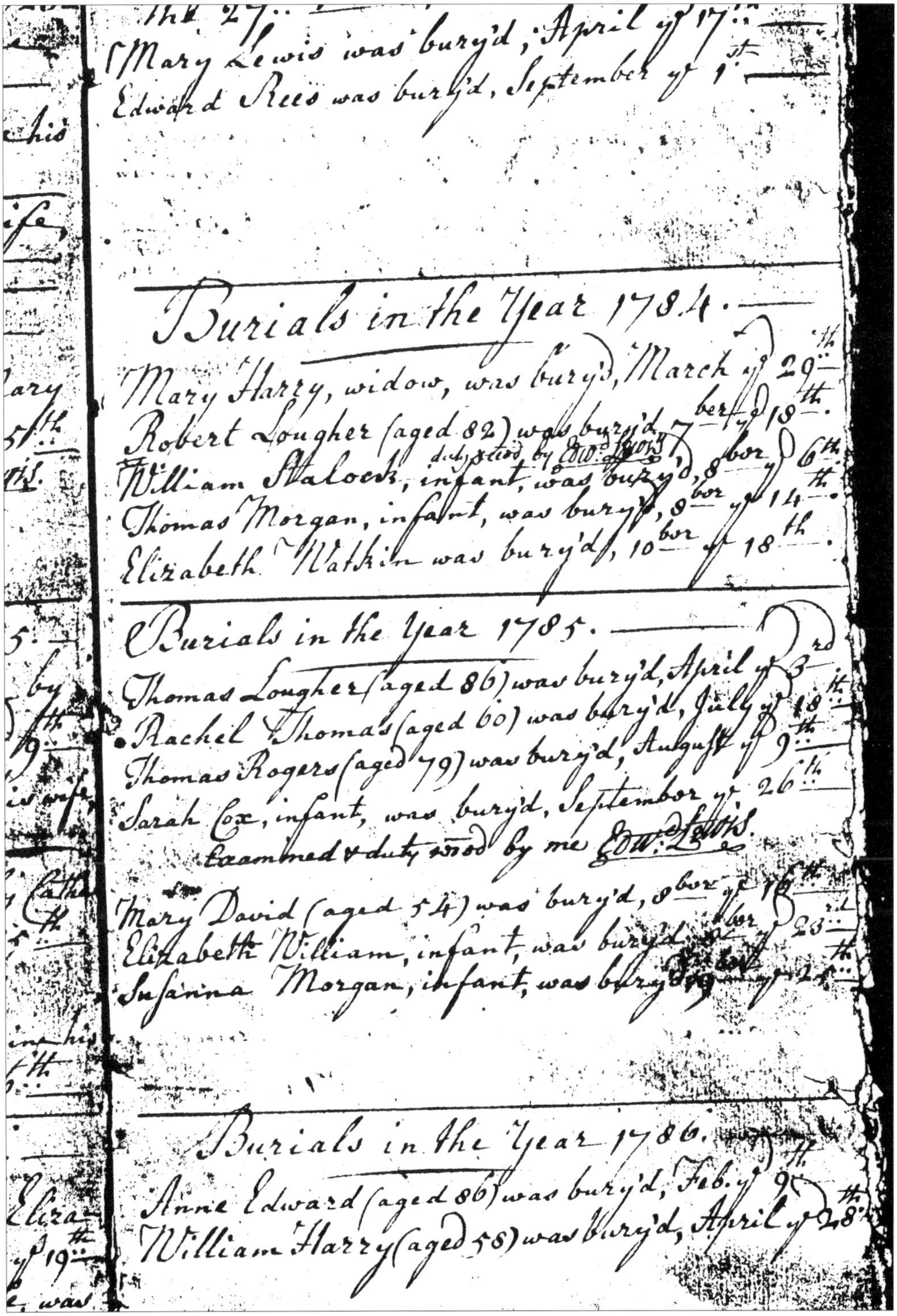

Mary Lewis was bury'd, April ye 17th
Edward Rees was bury'd, September ye 1st

Burials in the Year 1784.
Mary Harry, widow, was bury'd, March ye 29th
Robert Lougher (aged 82) was bury'd, 7ber ye 18th
duly [illegible] by Edw:d Lewis
William Staloch, infant, was bury'd, 8ber ye 6th
Thomas Morgan, infant, was bury'd, 8ber ye 14th
Elizabeth Watkin was bury'd, 10ber ye 18th

Burials in the Year 1785.
Thomas Lougher (aged 86) was bury'd, April ye 3rd
Rachel Thomas (aged 60) was bury'd, July ye 18th
Thomas Rogers (aged 79) was bury'd, August ye 9th
Sarah Cox, infant, was bury'd, September ye 26th
Examined & duly [illegible] by me Edw:d Lewis
Mary David (aged 54) was bury'd, 8ber ye 16th
Elizabeth William, infant, was bury'd, 9ber ye 23rd
Susanna Morgan, infant, was bury'd, 9ber ye 24th

Burials in the Year 1786.
Anne Edward (aged 86) was bury'd, Feb. ye 9th
William Harry (aged 58) was bury'd, April ye 28th

28. Entries in the parish register: Burials, 1783-86.
(Glamorgan Record Office.)

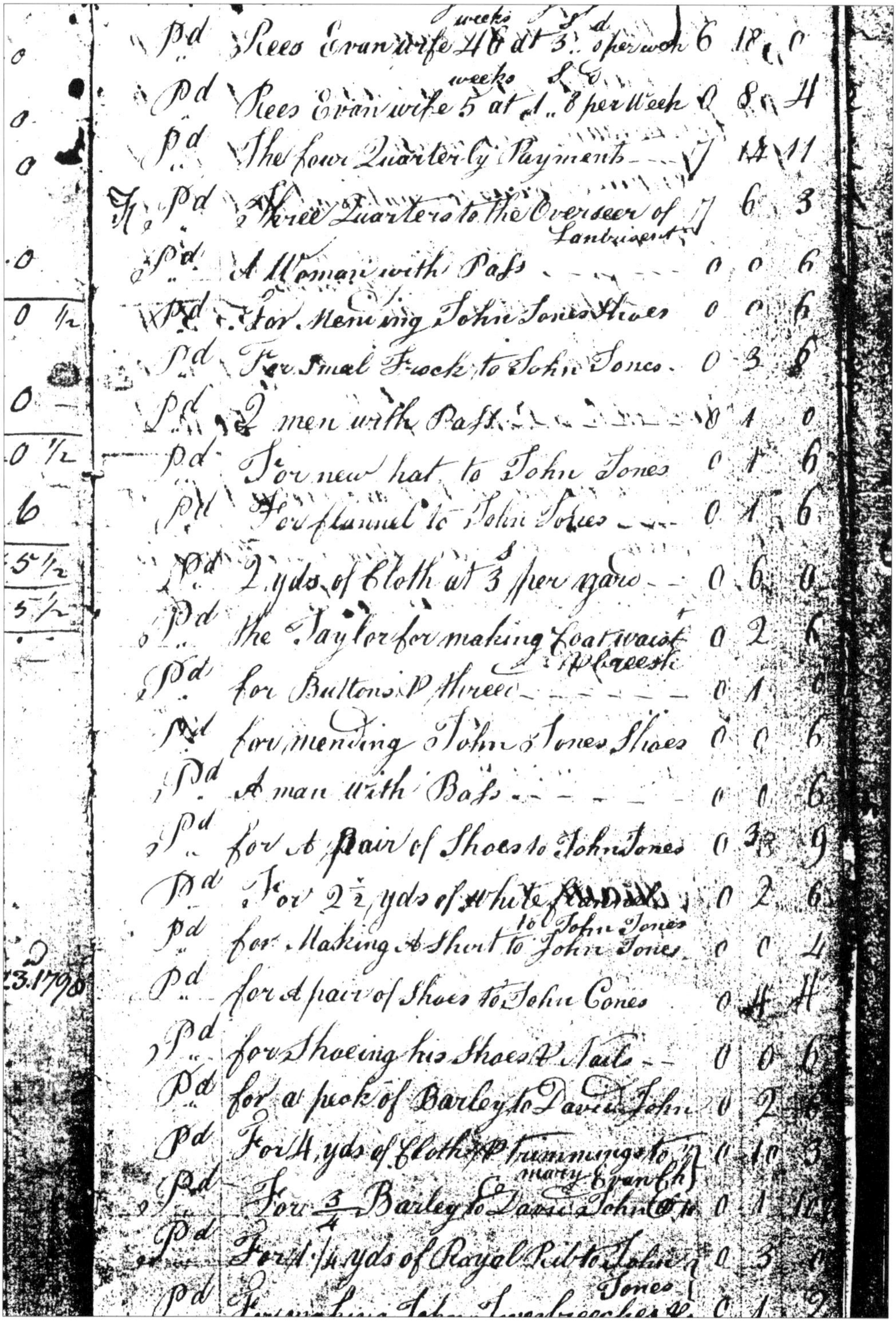
Pd Rees Evan wife 46 weeks at 3s 0d per week 6 18 0
Pd Rees Evan wife 5 weeks at 1s 8d per Week 0 8 4
Pd The four Quarterly Payments 7 14 11
Pd Three Quarters to the Overseer of Lantrisent 7 6 3
Pd A Woman with Pass 0 0 6
Pd For Mending John Jones Shoes 0 0 6
Pd For Smal Frock to John Jones 0 3 6
Pd 2 men with Pass 0 1 0
Pd For new hat to John Jones 0 1 6
Pd For flannel to John Jones 0 1 6
Pd 2 yds of Cloth at 3s per yard 0 6 0
Pd the Taylor for making Coat waist & Breeches 0 2 6
Pd for Buttons & thread 0 1 [illegible]
Pd for mending John Jones Shoes 0 0 6
Pd A man with Pass 0 0 6
Pd for A pair of Shoes to John Jones 0 3 9
Pd For 2½ yds of White flannel 0 2 6
Pd for Making A Shirt to John Jones 0 0 4
Pd for A pair of Shoes to John Jones 0 4 4
Pd for Shoeing his Shoes & Nails 0 0 6
Pd for a peck of Barley to David John 0 2 [illegible]
Pd For 4 yds of Cloth & trimmings to Mary Evan 0 10 3
Pd For ¾ Barley to David John 0 1 [illegible]
Pd For 4¼ yds of Rayal Rib to John Jones 0 3 [illegible]
Pd For making John Jones breeches & 0 1 [illegible]

29. Account of Francis Moris, overseer of the poor, 1798-99.
(Glamorgan Record Office.)

Care of the Poor

Overseers of the Poor were chosen from among the 'substantial householders' in the community and were elected at the annual vestry. Together with the churchwardens, whose main function was the maintenance of the church and churchyard, they were responsible for collecting the parish rate and for distributing it in accordance with the wishes of the parish vestry. Office was held for a year, but with the 'pool' of eligible office holders limited, the same names crop up time and again (usually after the decent interval of a year) and often one man (very occasionally in any parish a woman) will combine two or more offices, as for example in 1752 when Morgan David was churchwarden, petty constable and overseer of the poor, in 1753 when John How also occupied these three offices, and in 1758 when John Thomas served as overseer of the poor and churchwarden.

Richard Harry, overseer of the poor in 1733, was accountable for £1 18s 10½d., the proceeds of a parish rate levied at ½d. per acre, and during his year of office dispensed £1 15s. 0d. of that sum in poor relief. One of the major recipients was Margared Hugh who, having received payments of money and gifts of coal and wheat over a period of ten weeks, died a pauper and was buried 'on the parish'. Recorded in the accounts are sums totalling 2s. 2d. for digging the grave, paying two women, Maud Loughar and Susan Rees, for dressing the corpse and buying candles for Margared's watchnight.

The name of William Dyer alias Diar first appears in the parish accounts in May 1742, and thereafter for over ten years William was in receipt of parish relief. In the first few years he received one shilling a week, but by 1748 the weekly sum had been increased to half a crown [2s. 6d.] and was supplemented by hand-outs of clothing, blankets and rugs. When he died in 1753 William Diar was buried by the parish, his burial marked by the tolling of a church bell.

Responsibility for the care of the poor was a heavy burden upon a parish, and no parish was prepared, or indeed financially able, to support paupers who had no legal place of settlement within it. Enforcement of strict laws of settlement could involve a whole range of officials, from the parish constable who might arrest an unfortunate vagrant, to the justices of the peace who were empowered to issue Removal Orders authorising parish officials to send the vagrants back to their parish of legal settlement, often the parish of their birth.

As revealed in the St Hilary parish accounts, the overseer of the poor was the official most frequently charged with enforcing such Orders. For Richard Harry, in 1733, the removal of John Thomas and his family to St Mary Church involved little more than a short journey to the parish boundary and payment of 2s. 6d. for the Order. But for David William, overseer in 1797, a pauper vagrant and her family caused considerable work and expense. His account reveals that Mary Evan and her two children were removed from Bristol to St Hilary via Cardiff, and that this journey cost the parish over 20s. 0d.:

For a man and 2 horses to fetch Mary Evan and her 2 children from Cardiff	5s. 0d.
For 3 days boarding and lodging for do.	3s. 0d.
Also in Relief to do. to proceed on her journey	10s. 0d.
Also to pay part of house rent at Bristol	3s. 0d.

If earlier entries in the same account of payments of 16s. 0d. in relief to 'Rees Evans wife' relate to the same family a complex family story appears to lie hidden in the pages of this document. Once Mary and her children were back in St Hilary the parish became responsible for their maintenance. Four weeks 'keep' for the son who was probably boarded out and expected to work for his keep amounted to 6s. 0d. A pair of shoes for each child cost in total 4s. 8d.; the tapping of their mother's shoes cost 1s. 6d. What also appear in the account are two sums 'for Ale at a Vestry' when the affairs of Mary Evan were discussed by the parish officials. The ale cost 7s. 0d., more than a month's keep for the poor young boy.

Mary Evan's son was probably too young to be apprenticed thereby relieving the parish of his maintenance. But for many of these unfortunate children their fate was to be apprenticed to a trade which would, in theory, enable them to earn their own living in adulthood. In practice, many were handed over to local farmers to work as farm labourers or domestic servants and to a life of unremitting toil and poverty. What, one wonders, was the fate of young John Jones, fitted out in 1798 with shoes, breeches, coat, waistcoat and hat at parish expense before he became an apprentice?

Bastardy

Bastardy and the maintenance of bastard children also brought responsibilities to parish officials. The names of 'supposed' children of named individuals appear regularly in the annual lists of baptisms and in 1798, for example, out of a total of nine children baptised three were 'supposed' with the names of both parents being recorded. It was the identification and apprehension of fathers that often caused problems for the parish. The Settlement Act of 1732/3 made the fathers of bastard children responsible for their maintenance, and parish overseers by enforcing the legislation prevented the financial burden of providing for such children falling upon the parish.

Some fathers could prove singularly elusive. Morgan David, overseer of the poor in 1736, spent an inordinate amount of time and money in pursuit of one William Hary, father of Ann Morgan's bastard child. Having taken Ann Morgan to Penllyn to swear on oath before Reynold Deere, justice of the peace, that William Hary was indeed the father, the overseer then tried to find and apprehend the man. As his account reveals, he sought him here, there and everywhere, by day and by night, from Ewenny to Leckwith, from Aberthaw to Llantrisant. The search involved the co-operation and payment of parish officials in all these places, and only after days of searching and expenditure totalling over 15s. 0d. was William Hary finally apprehended at Leckwith. And the saga did not end there, for Morgan Wade, parish overseer in 1737, records in his account a payment of 2s. 6d. to one Cradock Evan 'for his trubul in taking William Hary'.

Occasionally the accounts reveal that humanity tempered legal and financial dictates. John How junior, overseer in 1796/7, paid 2s. 6d. to 'ten men in Distress Coming from Sea'. One of his predecessors in office made payments of a few pence to 'The little Boy' of whom nothing else is known.

Activities of Churchwardens

The activities of the churchwardens were also an integral part of village and parish life. Responsible with the vicar for the maintenance of the fabric of the church, their duties extended into many aspects of the life of St Hilary and beyond.

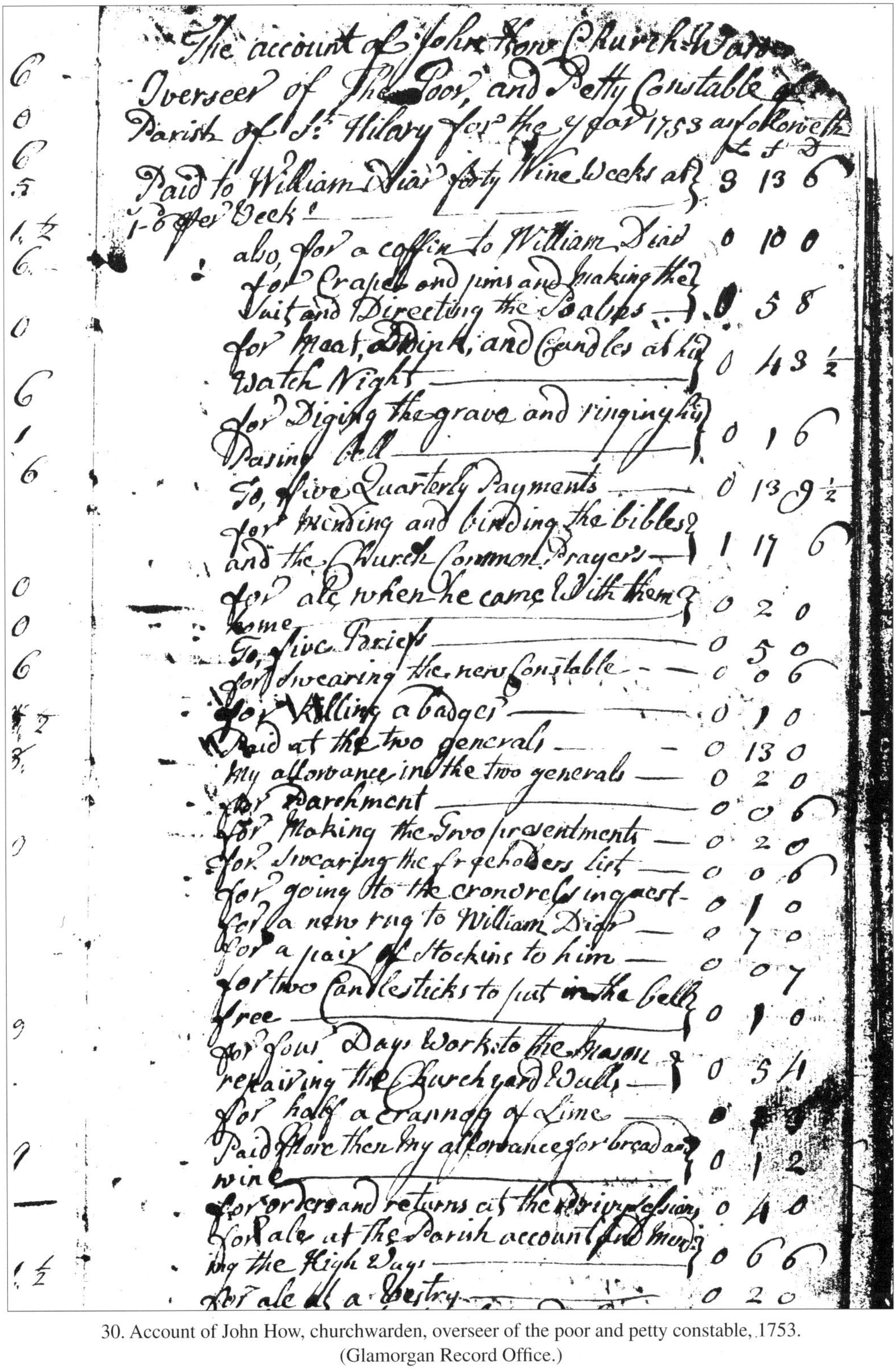
The account of John How Church Warden Overseer of the Poor, and Petty Constable of Parish of St Hilary for the year 1753 as followeth

	£	s	d
Paid to William Diar forty Nine Weeks at 1-6 per Week	3	13	6
also, for a coffin to William Diar	0	10	0
for Crapes and pins and making the Suit and Directing the Psalms	0	5	8
for Meat, Drink, and Candles at his Watch Night	0	4	3½
for Diging the grave and ringing his Pasing Bell	0	1	6
To, five Quarterly Payments	0	13	9½
for mending and binding the bibles and the Church Common Prayers	1	17	6
for ale when he came with them home	0	2	0
To, five [illegible]	0	5	0
for Swearing the new Constable	0	0	6
for killing a badger	0	1	0
Paid at the two generals	0	13	0
My allowance in the two generals	0	2	0
for parchment	0	0	6
for Making the Two presentments	0	2	0
for Swearing the freeholders list	0	0	6
for going to the cronorel's inquest	0	1	0
for a new rug to William Diar	0	7	0
for a pair of Stockins to him	0	0	7
for two Candlesticks to put in the belfree	0	1	0
for four Days Work to the Mason repairing the Churchyard Wall	0	5	4
for half a Crannock of Lime	[illegible]		
Paid More then my allowance for bread and wine	0	1	2
for orders and returns at the [illegible] sessions	0	4	0
for ale at the Parish account and mending the High Ways	0	6	6
for ale at a Vestry	0	2	0

30. Account of John How, churchwarden, overseer of the poor and petty constable, 1753. (Glamorgan Record Office.)

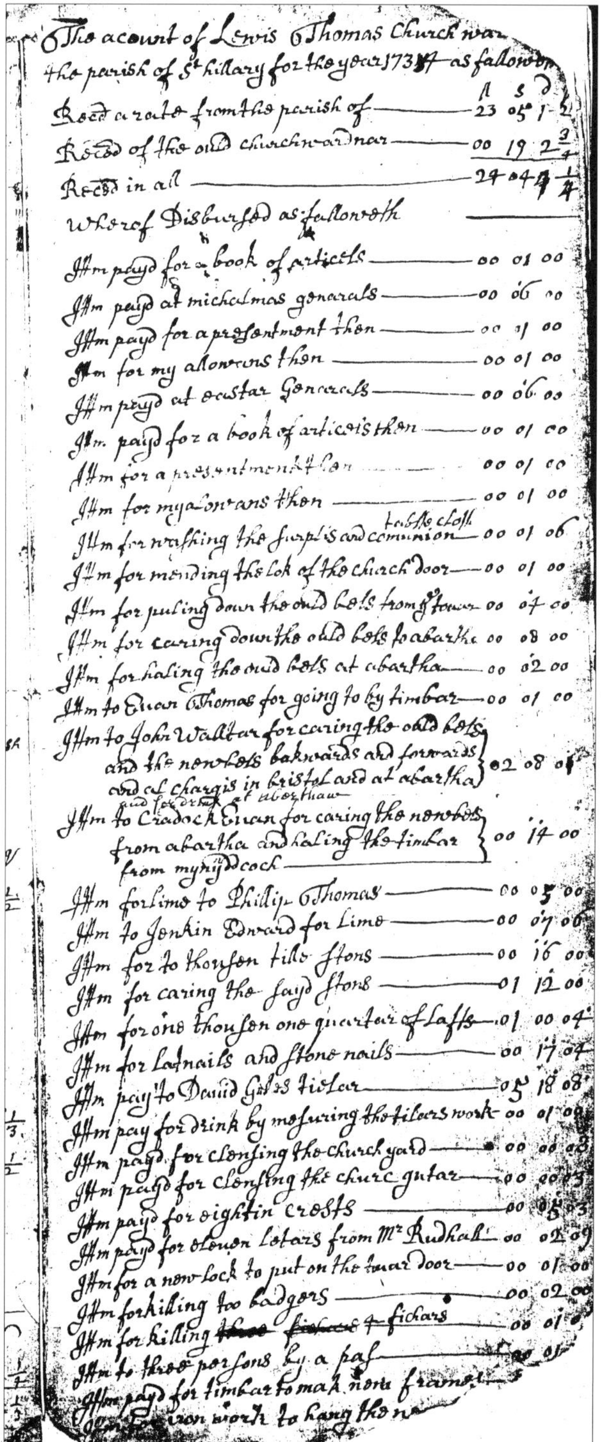

The acount of Lewis Thomas Church war[den]
the parish of St hillary for the year 1734 as falloweth

	li	s	d
Reced a rate from the parish of	23	05	1 ½
Reced of the old churchwardnar	00	19	2 ¾
Reced in all	24	04	4 ¼

Whereof Disbursed as falloweth

Item payd for a book of articels	00	01	00
Item payd at michalmas genarals	00	06	00
Item payd for a presentment then	00	01	00
Item for my alowans then	00	01	00
Item payd at eastar Genarals	00	06	00
Item payd for a book of articels then	00	01	00
Item for a presentment then	00	01	00
Item for my alowans then	00	01	00
Item for washing the surplis and comunion table cloth	00	01	06
Item for mending the lok of the church door	00	01	00
Item for puling down the ould bels from ye tower	00	04	00
Item for caring down the ould bels to abartha	00	08	00
Item for haling the ould bels at abartha	00	02	00
Item to Evan Thomas for going to by timbar	00	01	00
Item to John Wallbar for caring the ould bels and the new bels bakwards and forwards and al chargis in bristol and at abartha	02	08	0[illegible]
Item to Cradock Evan for caring the new bels and for drink at abarthaw from abartha and haling the timbar from mynyd cock	00	14	00
Item for lime to Phillip Thomas	00	05	00
Item to Jonkin Edward for Lime	00	07	06
Item for to thouson tile stons	00	16	00
Item for caring the sayd stons	01	12	00
Item for one thouson one quartar of lafts	01	00	04
Item for latnails and stone nails	00	17	04
Item pay to David Giles tilar	05	18	08
Item pay for drink by mesuring the tilers work	00	01	00
Item payd for clensing the church yard	00	00	0[illegible]
Item payd for clensing the churc gutar	00	00	[illegible]
Item payd for eightin crosts	00	0[illegible]	[illegible]
Item payd for eleven letars from Mr Rudhall	00	0[illegible]	09
Item for a new lock to put on the tower door	00	01	00
Item for killing too badgers	00	02	00
Item for killing ~~three fichars~~ 4 fichars	00	01	[illegible]
Item to three parsons by a pas	00	01	[illegible]
Item payd for timbar to mak new frame[s]			
[illegible] iron work to hang the ne[w bels]			

31. Account of Lewis Thomas, churchwarden, including payments for recasting the church bells, 1734. (Glamorgan Record Office.)

The first churchwarden who can be identified bore the surname Jenkin and held office in the year 1728. Regular disbursements by him and his successors included small sums for minor repairs and upkeep of the church—tiling, glazing, white liming, new locks and bell ropes. Provision of bread and wine for the communion, candles to illuminate the church during services, and brooms to sweep the church were other frequent items of expenditure. Washing of the church linen was entrusted to a local woman who was paid for her services. More exceptional items of expenditure recorded in the accounts include the sum of £2 3s. 0d. in 1727 (over half that year's church rate) for a 'Church Inglish bieble' and 'a Church Inglish Comon prayer book'. A decade later the latter volume was covered in 'green shage' by the tailor John Lewis at a cost to the parish of 2s. 4d. The Welsh Common Prayer Book was bound in 1743 at a cost of 6s. 0d.

The churchwardens' duties also extended to keeping the churchyard free from vermin, and in the accounts are regular payments of a few pence for killing creatures regarded as vermin, among them 'fitchets' [polecats], 'hedgocks' and badgers.

Year upon year the churchwardens attempted to ensure that the church was kept in a reasonable state of repair. Their resources were limited, they were dependent upon the expertise and competence of local carpenters, tilers, locksmiths, blacksmiths and others, and if by the middle of the nineteenth century St Hilary, like most of the Vale churches, was in great need of restoration, it is nevertheless to the credit of the parish that successive generations had grappled with the daunting task of maintaining the ancient building.

From time to time parish officials were faced with the oversight of exceptional projects, as in the 1730s when St Hilary embarked upon two ambitious schemes, the retiling of the church roof and the recasting of the church bells. The accounts which survive provide fascinating insights into the work, personalities and costs involved.

Both projects were financed out of the church rate which was increased substantially as work progressed. In 1730, a year of unexceptional expenditure, the rate was levied at 1½d. per acre and raised £5 13s. 7d. The following year, when large quantities of tiles and timber were purchased, the rate was charged at 5d. per acre to raise £19 8s. 9½d. And in 1734 and 1735, the years of the bells, sums in excess of £23 0s. 0d. were raised.

The first significant entry relating to the bells, records a sum of 2s. 6d. paid out by the churchwardens in 1730 'for drink when we looced to agree with the belfounder'. Subsequent entries reveal that the parish was in communication with a noted family of bellfounders, the Rudhalls of Gloucester, and that preparations were being made for the removal of the four bells from the tower and for their journey to Aberthaw and across the Bristol Channel en route to Gloucester. Items in the accounts for sawn timber, ropes, and for ladders to go up the tower give little indication of the magnitude of the task of 'puling down the oulde bels from ye towar' and ensuring their safe passage to and from the bellfounders. Wooden scaffolding as well as stout ladders, ropes and pulleys were needed to lower the bells before they could be gently manoeuvred onto specially constructed wooden cradles for the journey to Aberthaw. A small army of workmen must have been involved, as well as horses or oxen to haul the heavy loads to the coast. At Aberthaw the bells were put on board ship, carried across the water to Bristol and taken from there to Gloucester. Thomas Basset and Lewis Thomas, the churchwardens in 1734, supervised the operations and paid the various persons involved. John Waltar received £2 8s. 1d. 'for caring the ould bels and the new bels backwards and forwards and for all chargis at Bristol and at Abartha'. Cradock Evan, a former churchwarden, who also carted the new bells back to St Hilary from Aberthaw was paid 14s. 0d. Great must have been the rejoicing in

32. St Hilary Church Bells.

the parish when the bells rang out once more from the church tower. Each bell bore an inscription, together with the date of the recasting (1734), and engraved on the tenor bell were the names of the churchwardens Thomas Basset and Lewis Thomas. The following year their successor settled Rudhalls' bill for £20 11s. 0d. and the churchwardens' accounts revert to more mundane payments.

Eighteenth-Century Vicars and Parishioners

David Jones, vicar of St Hilary from 1723 to 1738, must have celebrated with his parishioners the safe return of the bells. He was succeeded by James Jones who died in office in 1750 and was himself succeeded by Henry Jones. Most of St Hilary's vicars until this date remain shadowy figures, but Henry Jones and his successor has each left his own strong imprint upon the history of the parish.

In 1758 the Reverend Henry Jones was brought before the diocesan court to answer charges of 'indecent and scandalous behaviour'. Complaints had been made to the Cathedral Chapter of the vicar's drunkenness, immorality, profane cursing and swearing, and on the evidence presented Jones was found guilty and forced to resign his living. His successor was the scholarly and conscientious John Walters, rector of Llandough and St Mary Church, who is now best remembered for his compilation and publication of a comprehensive English-Welsh dictionary, and whose reputation as cleric, scholar and *pater familias* was irreproachable.

The picture that emerges of St Hilary in the eighteenth century is that of a small, close-knit community, dependent in large measure upon its own resources to regulate its affairs, essentially a farming community with the majority of its population (145 in 1801) deriving a living from agriculture. The church remained the dominant focus of religious and social life in the village, unchallenged by nonconformist meeting houses. The only evidence of a dissenting presence in St Hilary is the registration, in 1748, of the house of Priscilla How as a meeting place for Quakers.

During the nineteenth century many aspects of village and parish life would be subtly altered. In the twentieth century the whole character of place and community would be transformed.

THE WIDER COMMUNITY IN THE EIGHTEENTH AND NINETEENTH CENTURIES

Law and Order / Crime and Punishment

Many of the minor quarrels and disturbances, much of rowdiness and malicious gossip that were part of village life were dealt with by the parish constable. Among the men who served this office in St Hilary in the eighteenth century were John Richard, Robert Nicholas, George Nicholas and Richard Hary, and although their accounts give tantalisingly few insights into local 'problems' one revealing entry occurs in the account of John Richard for 1734: 'Payd for mending the Stok [stocks] ls. 0d.' Punishment and humiliation, it seems, were meted out on the village green.

More serious offences were taken before the justices of the peace meeting in quarter sessions, or before the judges in great sessions or assizes. Few instances of criminal activity by inhabitants of St Hilary are to be found among the court records, and in this respect the parish was no better or worse than its neighbours where the majority of men and women lived out their lives in lawful obscurity.

Only on rare occasions was a crime deemed sufficiently heinous to merit the death penalty, but when this was the case the appointed place of execution was Stalling Down. The spectacle of the prisoner taken in a cart to the Down, guarded by the gaoler and his assistants, the presence of the hangman, and the sight of the gibbet silhouetted against the skyline lured spectators from across the Vale. For the inhabitants of St Hilary, these macabre dramas enacted on their very doorstep must have exerted a dreadful fascination.

One April morning in 1770 Henry Thomas was brought to Stalling Down to be hanged for the murder of Watkin Thomas of Boverton. In August 1778 Thomas Arthur was hanged for the murder of an old woman in Cardiff. On each occasion the corpse was carted away, that of Henry Thomas to be delivered to the surgeons for dissection, that of Thomas Arthur to be hung in chains on Mynydd Bychan in Cardiff.

John Thomas Hary was hanged on the Down in May 1786 after what seems to have been a particularly notorious criminal career, for he was convicted of theft, a crime which more usually earned a sentence not of death but of transportation. The event attracted the attention of the diarist William Thomas who wrote:

> 10 May 1786. Was Hanged on Stalling Down John Thomas Hary, of about 45 years old, that dreadfull thief, and his corps was set in a coffin and carryed to be buried to Eglwys Ilan, and great was the crowd that came to see his Death.

A few months later another thief was brought to the gallows, and it may be that Hopkin Thomas alias Bowen, a labourer from Llangyfelach convicted of stealing a mare and a gelding, had some connection with St Hilary. According to William Thomas, after the hanging on Stalling Down in September 1786 the body was taken to St Hilary for burial, but the parish register does not record the event.

The fate of two more malefactors is recorded by the diarist the following year:

> 20 April 1787. Were hanged on Stalling Down before the Judges left the Town of Cowbridge, William Owens, for the murder of Mary Haries his lover, and the man for killing his wife . . . A dismal tragedy. William Owens was about 23 years and the other 37 years old.

33. St Hilary and Stalling Down, as shown on Yates's map of Glamorgan, 1799. (Note that the site of the gallows is depicted on the northern edge of Stalling Down.)

The thirty-seven-year-old murderer was Cornelius Gordon of Llanrhidian, in Gower, who had killed his wife Mary (née Bevan) by battering her with a spade. An eye-witness account of his hanging is recorded in the notebooks of the antiquarian David Jones of Wallington (1834-90). He writes that an old lady, Mrs Howe of St Mary Church, told him that as a young child she had been taken up to Stalling Down to witness the execution of Gordon. Mrs Howe recalled the scene as Gordon's mother and family stood by with a coffin ready to take the body back to Llanrhidian for burial, and how, at the moment of execution 'the whole Down trembled . . . as with an earthquake.'

When St Hilary individuals do appear in court records the events are much less dramatic than those described above. The sudden death of Catherine Gwynn in St Hilary in 1774 necessitated an inquest conducted by the coroner and attended by the parish constable. In the same year Edward Rees of St Hilary, miller, was accused of stealing cordwood belonging to John Edmondes of Cowbridge from [Howe] Mill wood. The case was thrown out, but the charge had been brought by Edmondes who, a year later, purchased the Beaupre estate. Such litigation could scarcely have endeared him and his family to their new tenants.

Social Activities

For every level of Glamorgan society Cowbridge held its particular attractions. Some gentry families maintained a town house there in addition to their country properties, and attended balls and other social events at the Assembly Rooms and elsewhere in the town. Justices of the peace and judges met to dispense justice at the Town Hall or Bear Hotel. Farmers took their beasts to market, exchanged local intelligence and drank at the numerous public houses. Fair days attracted all sorts of traders and dealers, and for many country people Cowbridge on such days, crowded with people and animals, alive with noise and colour, crammed with booths and stalls, must have been an irresistible lure, a magnet of novelty and excitement.

For most farm workers and their families in St Hilary, as elsewhere in the Vale, life was marked by unceasing toil, familiarity with death, and the prospect of infirmity and poverty in old age. Even a visit to Cowbridge was a rare treat, and in such circumstances the smallest pleasurable diversions were seized—visits of itinerant pedlars and musicians to the parish, wedding celebrations, harvest suppers, a jar of ale quaffed in the smoke-filled room of The Bush. Many a foot in St Hilary must have tapped and danced to the music of Thomas Lewis of Howe Mill (Thomas o Felynhydd) who, according to the diarist William Thomas, was regarded as the best fiddler in Glamorgan until his death and burial in St Hilary in May 1763.

The image of Stalling Down as a place of execution is a potent one, but the expanse of open land encompassing St Hilary Down and Stalling Down was, more usually, a place where people enjoyed themselves, a venue for horse racing and foot races. Such events attracted participants and spectators from far afield as well as from the Vale and, as on market and fair days, the gathering of people and animals would have created a noisy, busy, indeed often riotous assembly.

From the pages of William Thomas' diary one can obtain a sense of the excitement that pervaded these occasions:

> 27 and 28 Sep.1765. Horse races on the Stalling Down and much Noise and Rioting everywhere about this month.

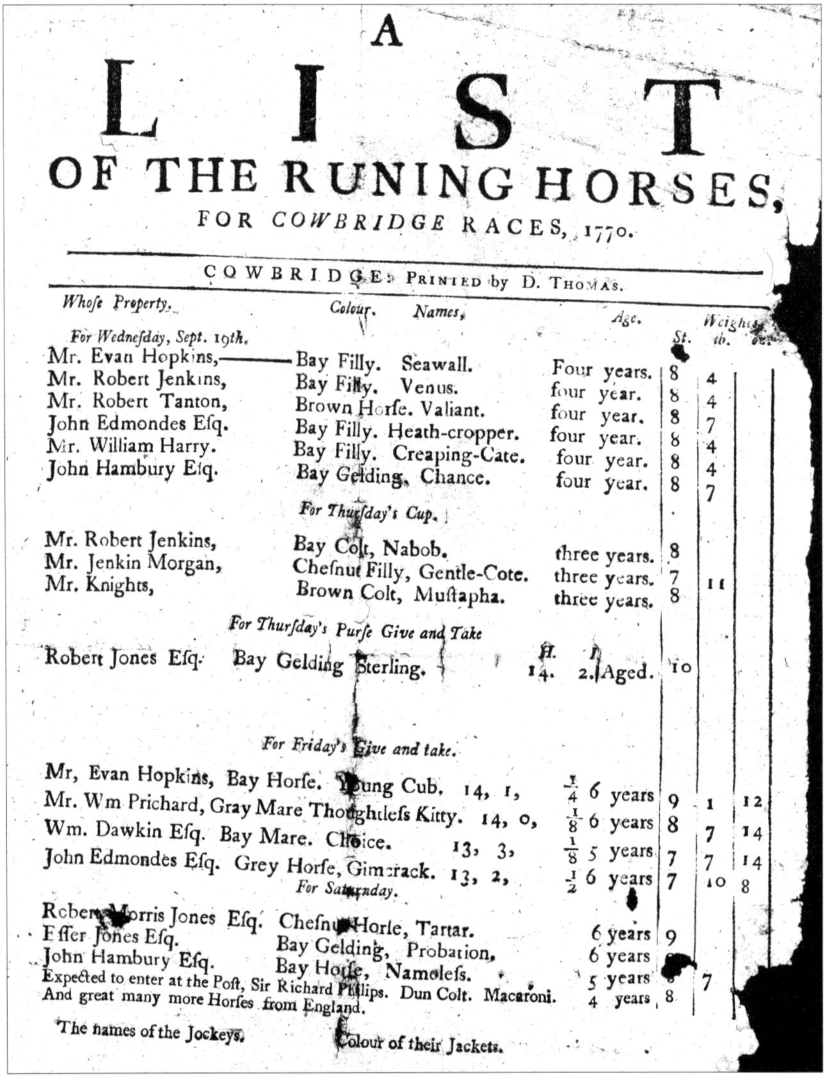

A
LIST
OF THE RUNING HORSES,
FOR *COWBRIDGE* RACES, 1770.

COWBRIDGE: PRINTED by D. THOMAS.

Whose Property.	*Colour.*	*Names,*	*Age.*	*St.*	*lb.*	
For Wednesday, Sept. 19th.						
Mr. Evan Hopkins,—	Bay Filly.	Seawall.	Four years.	8	4	
Mr. Robert Jenkins,	Bay Filly.	Venus.	four year.	8	4	
Mr. Robert Tanton,	Brown Horse.	Valiant.	four year.	8	7	
John Edmondes Esq.	Bay Filly.	Heath-cropper.	four year.	8	4	
Mr. William Harry.	Bay Filly.	Creaping-Cate.	four year.	8	4	
John Hambury Esq.	Bay Gelding,	Chance.	four year.	8	7	
For Thursday's Cup.						
Mr. Robert Jenkins,	Bay Colt,	Nabob.	three years.	8		
Mr. Jenkin Morgan,	Chesnut Filly,	Gentle-Cote.	three years.	7	11	
Mr. Knights,	Brown Colt,	Mustapha.	three years.	8		
For Thursday's Purse Give and Take						
Robert Jones Esq.	Bay Gelding	Sterling. *H.* 14. *I.* 2.	Aged.	10		
For Friday's Give and take.						
Mr, Evan Hopkins,	Bay Horse.	Young Cub. 14, 1, $\frac{1}{4}$	6 years	9	1	12
Mr. Wm Prichard,	Gray Mare	Thoughtless Kitty. 14, 0, $\frac{1}{8}$	6 years	8	7	14
Wm. Dawkin Esq.	Bay Mare.	Choice. 13, 3, $\frac{1}{8}$	5 years	7	7	14
John Edmondes Esq.	Grey Horse,	Gimcrack. 13, 2, $\frac{1}{2}$	6 years	7	10	8
For Saturday.						
Robert Morris Jones Esq.	Chesnut Horse,	Tartar.	6 years	9		
Esser Jones Esq.	Bay Gelding,	Probation,	6 years			
John Hambury Esq.	Bay Horse,	Nameless.	5 years	8	7	
Expected to enter at the Post, Sir Richard Philips.	Dun Colt.	Macaroni.	4 years	8		

And great many more Horses from England.

The names of the Jockeys. Colour of their Jackets.

34. Notice of Cowbridge Races, 1770.

Ever the moralist, William Thomas could not resist adding 'All driving to Ruining and poverty.' The following year events gave him even greater cause for comment:

> 4-6 June 1766. Horse races on the Stalling Down and much noise about them by the vulgar, from Corps Candles and Lights seen by nights as they report (which was nothing but men trying their horses on the Course by nights) . . . Here horses from Yorkshire, Carmarthenshire and several other parts, with a very great croud every day. Cock fightings and assemblies in the Town of Cowbridge.

If the diarist is to be believed much 'noise and riot', drunken revelry and fighting attended all such occasions.

How many St Hilary parishioners staggered home from these events? How exercised were the parish constables to maintain the peace? How many wagers were placed and lost? Even those who stayed at home must have been caught up in the excitement as sounds of pounding hooves and the clamour of the crowds drifted across the village.

An altogether quieter but nonetheless dramatic event which took place on the Down in 1829 had a particular significance for the people of St Hilary. Many of them would remember their former vicar, the Reverend John Walters, and his family including his younger son Henry. Talented but, as he grew older, increasingly eccentric, Henry Walters amassed a considerable library of books and manuscripts. 'The Cowbridge hermit' as he was known, died in 1829, and soon after his death his books and papers were carted up to Stalling Down and destroyed in a great bonfire.

All the events described above cast their shadow upon St Hilary and, indirectly, made their own contribution to the history of the place and its people.

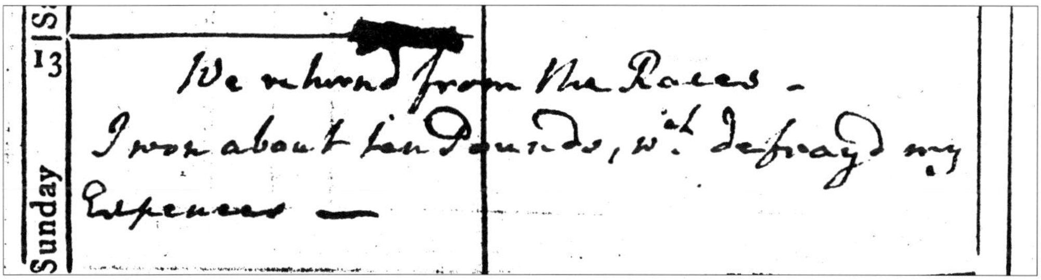
S 13 Sunday

We returned from the Races -
I won about ten Pounds, w.ch defray'd my
Expences —

Diary entry by the Reverend John Carne of Nash Manor recording his winnings at Cowbridge Races, 1771.
(Glamorgan Record Office.)

35. Old Beaupre farmhouse (photographed 1998).

36. The Cottage in the early C19th.

LANDOWNERS IN THE EIGHTEENTH AND NINETEENTH CENTURIES

After the sale of the Beaupre estate by the Bassets in 1709 the property passed through a rapid succession of owners and mortgagees until, in 1755, it was purchased by Thomas Edmondes of Old Hall, Cowbridge.

Having risen from trade into the ranks of estate stewards and lawyers, the Edmondes are a prime example of a nouveau riche family thrusting their way into gentry society through the acquisition of their own landed estate. The purchase by Thomas Edmondes of 'the manors of Beaupre and St Hilary' (as the property is described in the deed of purchase), amply fulfilled the social ambitions of the family, members of which could now divide their time between their 'town house' in Cowbridge and their 'country seat' in St Hilary.

Old Beaupre, already a picturesque ruin, its one habitable wing occupied by a farmer, was an unfit residence for its new owners and it was at Great House (the property later called The Manor) that John Edmondes, eldest son of Thomas, and his family established themselves. John Edmondes died at the early age of thirty-eight in 1778 leaving a widow, Margaret, and several young children, and the fact that a considerable quantity of his household furniture in his Cowbridge residence was sold soon after his death suggests that St Hilary became the main home of his widow and children.

John Edmondes had married twice. By his first wife Charlotte (née Dive) he had two daughters, Charlotte and Anna Maria, and it was through Charlotte's marriage to Llewellyn Traherne of Coedriglan in 1787 that the St Hilary/Beaupre estate passed into the hands of the Traherne family. By his second wife Margaret (née Deere) John Edmondes had a son and heir, Thomas, whose descendants were associated with Old Hall, and three more daughters.

In December 1796, Margaret Edmondes, then described as 'of Cowbridge', conveyed Great House, St Hilary, to her spinster step-daughter Anna Maria and to Llewellyn Traherne the recently widowed husband of her other step-daughter Charlotte. A son, John Montgomery, and three daughters, Charlotte, Louisa and Eleanor, had been born to Charlotte and Llewellyn Traherne, and after their mother's death the children were taken to live in St Hilary with their aunt. There, for a few short years, they were in charge of a governess and received tuition from a Monsieur Bonsil who taught them French and from Thomas Rhys of the Eagle Academy in Cowbridge who taught them handwriting.

After his second marriage, in 1798, to Barbara Manning, and the birth of his second son George, Llewellyn Traherne lived more permanently at Coedriglan, and the St Hilary house came to provide a home for his two unmarried daughters Charlotte and Louisa. But it was at St Hilary that Llewellyn Traherne died in 1841 having been cared for in his later years by those daughters.

Charlotte and Louisa Traherne continued to live in St Hilary after their father's death, but in the 1850s family disputes and a quarrel with their brother John Montgomery Traherne (1788-1860) and his wife Charlotte (née Talbot) led to their departure from The Manor, and to the refurbishment of the house for occupation by their brother and his wife. John Montgomery Traherne died at The Manor in February 1860. His sister Louisa ended her days in The Cottage ten years later.

The Cottage, in fact an elegant Regency villa, was home to the Reverend George Traherne and his family during his years (1832-53) as vicar of St Hilary. The house was probably built for him. The other Traherne residences in Glamorgan, Castellau in

37. The Reverend John Montgomery Traherne FRS, FSA (1788-1860).
(Illustration reproduced from *Glamorgan Historian* vol. 4, with kind permission of Stewart Williams.)

38. The Clump on St Hilary Down, photographed 1930s.
(Possibly of ancient origin, The Clump was planted by the Reverend J. M. Traherne early in the nineteenth century. It was replanted in 1990 as part of the St Hilary 900 celebrations.)

Llantrisant and Coedriglan alias Coedarhydyglyn in St George-super-Ely, are of similar design and it is known that the latter was built for the Reverend George's half-brother John Montgomery Traherne in the early 1820s. Photographs of The Cottage taken at the turn of the century suggest that an earlier, modestly proportioned house or 'cottage' was incorporated into the fabric of the villa.

Both John Montgomery Traherne and his half-brother George entered the church. Poor health determined that John's clerical career, during which he served as curate in St Hilary and was chancellor of the diocese of Llandaff, was brief and undistinguished, and it is as a man of broad scientific and antiquarian interests that he is best remembered. In the particular context of St Hilary he is credited with planting the circle of trees 'The Clump' on the highest point of the Down to commemorate the battle of Waterloo. His latter years were clouded by a succession of family disputes, and his quarrel with his half-brother George and with his nephew George Montgomery Traherne immediately affected the latter's expectations of inheritance. While the Coedriglan estate was secured to George Montgomery, the major part of the St Hilary estate under the terms of John Montgomery Traherne's Will passed to his godson, Llewelyn Traherne Basset Saunderson, whose family home was at Cavan, in Ireland.

Just over sixty years earlier, in May 1797, Llewellyn Traherne and his sister-in-law had sold off the Beaupre part of the St Hilary estate. Described as 'the manor, capital messuage, mills and farm called Beaupre' and comprising the old house and 500 acres of land, the property had been sold to a wealthy lawyer from Llantwit Major, Daniel Jones. Whether or not Beaupre was, or ever had been, a manor in its own right remains an open question, but what this sale unquestionably did was to wrench Beaupre from its ancient association with the wider St Hilary estate. Yet, by a quirk of fate, its sale to Daniel Jones paved the way for its re-association with the family of Basset.

Among the monuments in St Hilary church is one to Daniel Jones of Beaupre, his likeness sculpted above an inscription testifying to his philanthropic works, notably his role as a founder benefactor of the Cardiff Royal Infirmary. In the grandiloquent words of the memorial, he was also responsible for restoring 'in the person of the son the ancient patrimony of their family'. The patrimony was Beaupre and the family that of Basset. Daniel Jones died, childless, in 1841. He had married a daughter of Whitlock Nicholl of Ham, Llantwit Major, but some instinct prompted him to leave his estate not to a member of the family but to the then representative of the Bassets of Beaupre, Richard Basset. And from that date the Bassets became closely associated once again with Beaupre, taking up residence in New Beaupre, the house built by Daniel Jones a short distance to the north of the old ancestral mansion.

Richard Basset's tenure of Beaupre was brief, for he died in November 1849 at the age of fifty-one. His tomb stands within a railed enclosure in the churchyard and, in addition to the family coat of arms and motto, bears the inscription 'last male heir of the ancient family of Basset of Beaupre'. His widow, Frances, continued to reside at New Beaupre until her death in 1865 when she was buried alongside her husband. The estate then passed to their nephew, Major William West James Bruce (d.1871) who, on succeeding to the property, assumed the surname of Basset. His tomb stands within the family's enclosure in the churchyard and he is also commemorated by a marble monument in the church, a monument, which like that of Daniel Jones, incorporates a sculpted likeness of the deceased. Another memorial to uncle and nephew takes the form of a stained-glass window in the church.

39. Memorial tablet in the church commemorating Daniel Jones of Beaupre (d. 1841).

40. Basset family churchyard tombs: Richard Basset (d. 1849)
'last male heir of the ancient family of Basset of Beaupre'.

Bassets, Trahernes and Edmondeses maintained their links with St Hilary into the twentieth century. Other ancient landowners also retained their footholds in the parish. The Llandaff Cathedral Chapter held onto the glebe lands until the 1870s, while 'The Lake' and other lands on the western edge of the parish, long part of the Margam estate, remained in the ownership of the Mansel Talbot family until the late nineteenth/early twentieth century. But by the end of the nineteenth century new names were appearing among the residents of the village, among them Tyler, Penrose, Ackland-Allen and Franklen.

Major William West James Basset.
(Detail from church monument.)

41. South porch of St Hilary church (photographed 1998).

NINETEENTH-CENTURY CHURCH RESTORATION

A fine series of brass plaques, marble memorials and stained-glass windows in the church commemorate Edmondeses, Trahernes and latter-day Bassets. The church itself bears the heavy imprint of Victorian restoration, and the fact that the work of restoration was entrusted to the eminent architect Sir George Gilbert Scott ensured a high standard of workmanship and a true concern for the preservation of the ancient fabric of the building. The antiquarian interests of the Reverend J. M. Traherne had prompted him, in his latter years, to draw up plans for the restoration, and after his death in 1860 his widow, Charlotte, ensured that the project was carried out in his memory.

There is no doubt that by the mid-nineteenth century the church was in urgent need of repair. The Reverend Lewis Morgan, launching an appeal for funds in 1855, pointed to earlier, unsatisfactory improvements—'the ruthless hand of time has been arrested at different periods, doubtless by well-intentioned but mostly destructive repairs'—and he lamented the fact that such unsympathetic attempts at refurbishment had obliterated 'many of those traditional associations with the past, every vestige of which however simple or homely it may be, has the strongest claims upon our reverence and care.'

In its vicar who urged the preservation and restoration of whatever did still survive from the medieval building, in its architect who demonstrated a real concern to preserve such ancient features, and in Charlotte Traherne who bore the major costs of restoration, St Hilary was singularly fortunate. Craftsmen who had worked under Scott on other restoration projects, projects which included Westminster Abbey and St David's Cathedral, were employed on work for St Hilary, and in 1862 restoration was completed. Among the more notable features of the restored building are the south porch, designed by Scott

42. The interior of St Hilary church (photographed 1998).

himself to replace the original fourteenth-century and much decayed structure, and the magnificent east window where the hand of the architect is evident. The preservation of the two medieval effigies in the church owes much to their skilfull repair and cleaning at this time, work paid for by Mrs Frances Basset of New Beaupre.

It was not until 1875 that St Hilary was provided with a vicarage. One of the poorest livings in the Vale, it was frequently held 'in plurality' with its vicar living in one of his other parishes and leaving the care of souls in St Hilary to a curate. The Reverend John Walters, for example, who was also rector of Llandough and St Mary Church at the end of the eighteenth century, lived at Llandough. At the beginning of the nineteenth century the then vicar of St Hilary, the Reverend George Traherne who was also rector of St George-super-Ely, had his own private residence in the village. But by the latter decades of the century the need for a purpose-built vicarage was recognised and the Bonvilston architect, David Vaughan, prepared the plans. Part of the cost of building the 'parsonage house', estimated at £1800, was met by the sale of glebe lands. In 1875 The Vicarage was ready for occupation and the then vicar, the Reverend Lewis Morgan, moved from Bonvilston to St Hilary. The parish had waited long for its own vicarage, but within fifty years the house passed into lay ownership and Lewis Morgan was the first of only three incumbents to live there.

At the end of the nineteenth century St Hilary was provided with a well-restored church and an impressive new vicarage. And, in the wake of the 1862 restoration, the church benefited from a number of memorial bequests and donations. The magnificent reredos with its representation of the Last Supper was erected in memory of Samuel Devonsher Penrose (d.1872) by his widow. The churchyard lychgate was built in 1900 as a memorial to George Montgomery Traherne (d. 1896) by his widow Harriet Traherne. The tower screen was put up by parishioners and friends in memory of the Reverend Henry Charles Davies (rector 1892-1911). Since 1900 successive programmes of repair and maintenance have kept the fabric of the church in a sound state and, at the beginning of the twenty-first century, a regular pattern of worship is sustained within its walls.

Lychgate.

43. The Vicarage (later The Grange), *c.*1920.

44. St Hilary churchyard and lychgate with the old village school (now the village hall) in the background (photographed 1998).

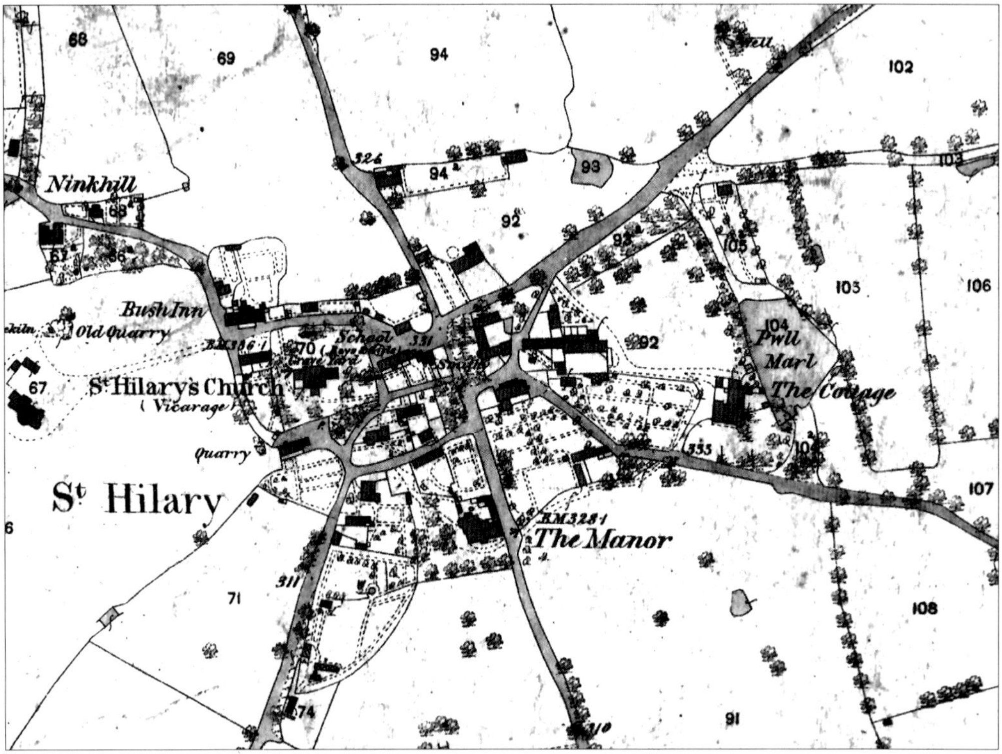

45. The village in 1877.
(Detail from Ordnance Survey map, Glamorgan sheet XLV.8)

46. Howe Mill, *c.*1890.

THE COMMUNITY IN THE NINETEENTH CENTURY

Throughout the nineteenth century St Hilary remained, essentially, what it had been for many centuries, a small, rural community with the majority of its inhabitants deriving an income from agriculture and associated trades. The size of the population varied little from decade to decade—145 in 1801, 157 in 1851, 175 in 1891—and was composed largely of farmers, agricultural labourers, domestic and farm servants and rural craftsmen.

The largest of the farms, The Farm alias Village Farm, with its old farmhouse and farm buildings in the heart of the village, comprised some 600 acres, and was the home of the Thomas family. Coed Hills, known as Cole Hills in the previous century, was farmed by generations of the David alias Davies family until, in the 1890s, it passed to farmer Edward Thomas. Old Beaupre was occupied by William Thomas in the 1850s and 1860s and thereafter by John alias Thomas Jones. Howe Mill and its lands (90 acres) passed through the hands of a succession of miller farmers, among them Morgan Thomas, Henry Braddick and David James.

Each of the farms in the parish employed varying numbers of farm and domestic servants thereby providing livelihoods for many village families. At Old Beaupre farm (140 acres) farmer Jones had two spinster sisters to help with farm and house work, and employed just two 'live in' servants, a young girl to work in the house and a young farm boy. By contrast, the household of widower farmer Thomas Thomas of Village Farm was impressive. Under the same roof with him and his two sons lived a housekeeper, two domestic servants and five farm servants, and the Thomases employed an additional thirteen men and a boy on the farm as work demanded. The Davieses at Coed Hills (100 acres in 1861) usually had a couple of farm servants living in, and in the 1850s and 1860s were employing five men on the farm. They, like their neighbours, would have employed casual workers at harvest and other busy seasons.

Cottages in the village provided homes for some twenty or more families, including those of a number of agricultural labourers who worked on the local farms. Here also lived the blacksmiths and wheelwrights, the thatchers, carpenters and masons whose skills were an essential element in the rural economy. And in several of the cottages a widow eked out a living as seamstress or laundress. Among those who can be identified in the second half of the nineteenth century are Edward Williams and his son Thomas, thatchers, George Watts and other members of the Watts family, blacksmiths, the brothers Edward and William Williams, wheelwrights, Henry Preston and Evan Cox, carpenters, John Morgan, mason. The widow Caroline Williams worked as a seamstress. Mary Russell, widow of one of the village carpenters, took in laundry. It is interesting to note that not all the village craftsmen were 'local'. George Watts who was still working in his smithy in 1881 aged seventy-five came originally from Wiltshire, other members of the Watts family from Gloucestershire. The Preston family hailed from Devon, and included Henry the village carpenter, and William who progressed from 'head gardener' at one of the gentry houses in 1871 to farmer in his own right at East Down by 1881.

Most of the cottages would have been small, some just two rooms, some 'two up and two down', and would often have accommodated large families. In 1871 William Rosser, agricultural labourer, was living in one of the cottages with his wife and seven children whose ages ranged from seventeen years to eight months. At the same date another cottage was occupied by David Williams, labourer, his wife Ann and five of their children, the eldest aged twenty-four the youngest twelve. Ten years later Ann was a widow but

47. Tyr Eglwys (later Abbotswood), with Mrs Ann Williams and her daughters Mary, Ann and Catherine, *c.*1880.

48. The Glebe farmhouse and Wendy Cottage, *c.*1890.

49. Myrtle Cottage with Jack Eddolls and his wife Elizabeth, *c.*1920.

50. The Manor house in the early C20th.

51. The Cottage in the early C20th.

apparently living comfortably, for she is described as farming six acres of land; her unmarried daughter Catherine had employment as a servant, her two bachelor sons were wheelwrights, and all three lived at home with their mother.

The 'big houses' played an important role in providing local employment. As befitted a widow of independent means, Charlotte Traherne (d. 1880) at the Great House employed a retinue of servants including housekeeper, lady's maid, cook, butler, footboy, kitchenmaid and housemaid. The Bassets at New Beaupre had a similarly impressive household staff supplemented by nurses and governesses for their young children. The Vicarage also had its servants; the Reverend Lewis Morgan, the first occupant of the house, employed four young women, two of them from St Hilary. The gentry, with wide social contacts, and with other town and country houses to maintain, often drew their 'live in' servants from all over the country, as did Charlotte Traherne. In 1871 her housekeeper was from London, her lady's maid, cook, butler and kitchenmaid had origins in Wiltshire, Oxfordshire, Carmarthenshire and Gower. But some of the household servants at the Great House were recruited from St Hilary and the adjacent parishes, and some of the outdoor staff both 'local' and 'incomers' were housed in estate cottages or were boarded out in the village. Rarely is it possible in this period (1800-1900) to determine who lived in a particular cottage, but in 1861 Pwll y Marl can be identified as the home of Thomas Llewellyn, agricultural labourer, his wife and five young children, and in 1891 Rose Cottage was occupied by John Morgan, mason, and his family, Nincil by William Hopkin, labourer, his wife and child.

The occupants of the big houses in addition to providing employment and housing also assumed the role of local benefactors. The Traherne family, for example, are known to have supported a school for poor children in St Hilary in the 1830s and 1840s and to have made generous donations to the church. Towards the end of the century village children looked forward to the Christmas party given for them at The Cottage by Mrs Harriet Traherne. A huge Christmas tree in the servants' hall, a laden table and 'useful' presents (sewing boxes for the girls, tools for the boys) and an orange for each child as they left were all part of this special treat. Most vivid in one small girl's memory was the sight of the butler extinguishing the candles with a sponge on the end of a pole!

Superficially, the village at the end of the nineteenth century appeared little changed from what it had been a century earlier. New tenants occupied some of the big houses in the village, among them Lieutenant Colonel John Hobart Tyler, JP, member of the Cottrell family, at The Manor, and Thomas Mansel Franklen at The Cottage, but their role as local gentry, like that of the Bassets, Trahernes and Saundersons, seemed unassailable. Farmers, cowkeepers, graziers, a miller and a blacksmith head a list of 'commercial residents' in a Directory of 1891, and the majority of the population continued to be employed on the land or in domestic service. But a few entries in the 1891 Census give glimpses of change. William Bennell, living at Beaupre Cottage, is described as 'foreman of excavators'; a village schoolmistress, Harriet Rogers, is lodging at Village Farm; there is a post office in the village.

The excavators were working on the Aberthaw Branch of the Taff Vale Railway which cut through St Hilary near Beaupre. Harriet Rogers was teaching at the National School (established 1856) which had accommodation for forty pupils. The village post office, located in Manor Cottage, was being run by the widow Mrs Anna Maria Poole who shared the property with her brother Orlando Watts the village blacksmith. Mrs Poole also taught at the school.

52. St Hilary schoolchildren with their teacher Miss Harriet Rogers and Mrs Poole, *c.*1880.

53. St Hilary schoolchildren with Miss Harriet Rogers, 1885.
From left to right: *(Back row)* James Denbury, Charlie Morgan, Davy Thomas, Charlie Howell, Davy Hopkin, Willie Thomas, John Denbury;
(Middle row) Annie Howell, Annie Morgan, Willie David, Daniel David, Jas Regan, Davy Morgan, Maria Morgan, Rhoda Thomas, Lizzie Howell, Miss Rogers;
(Front row) Windsor Howell, John Thomas, Cath Hopkins, Ellen Thomas, Lizzie Davies, Janie Morgan, Hannah Davies, Celia Hopkins, Sidney Morgan.

School, railway and post office represented change and progress and added new dimensions to village and parish life. But as the nineteenth century drew to its close few could have envisaged the pace and fundamental nature of change that was on the horizon.

One man whose life spanned the certainties of the old century and the upheavals of the new was Thomas Mansel Franklen (1840-1928). A member of the family which owned the Clemenston estate, Franklen was a barrister who practised on the South Wales circuit. In 1878 he became clerk of the peace for Glamorgan and in 1889 was appointed clerk of the newly created Glamorgan County Council, an office he held until his death. He was knighted in 1921. After his marriage to Florence Allen of Pembrokeshire he took up residence at The Cottage, St Hilary, and it was here that he lived until his death in 1928, when he was buried alongside his ancestors in Llandow churchyard. A man of great integrity and wide interests, Franklen was a generous benefactor of Cowbridge Grammar School and of church restoration schemes, he had an informed interest in archaeology and history, in horticulture and agriculture, and was an accomplished photographer. In the latter context he has left behind a superb collection of photographs of historic buildings in Glamorgan. Thomas Mansel Franklen and his wife had no children, but the family connection with St Hilary was and is maintained by their Ackland-Allen relations and through them by the Giles family. Although Franklen has no memorial in St Hilary, his name appears on one of the church bells, for when the bells were recast in 1906 a new bell was added, and on it were inscribed the names of the then churchwarden and vicar—Thomas Mansel Franklen and the Reverend Henry Charles Davies.

54. Sir Thomas Mansel Franklen (1840-1928).
(Glamorgan Record Office.)

55. Village children and Venom the dog, Primrose Day, 19 April 1886. (Photograph probably taken by Thomas Mansel Franklen.)

ST HILARY IN THE TWENTIETH CENTURY

Change and development

At the opening of the new century the Traherne and Edmondes families still retained land and property in St Hilary, but the major landowners were now the Bassets and the Saundersons. A number of large houses superfluous to the residential needs of their owners were let to tenants among whom, in 1906, were Thomas Mansel Franklen at The Cottage, Major C. R. H. Nicholl at The Manor House and Charles Ackland-Allen at The Cross. New Beaupre was occupied by Colonel Windham Henry Wyndham Quin (later 5th Earl of Dunraven), MP for the South Glamorgan parliamentary constituency from 1895 until his defeat in the General Election of 1906. Such well-connected individuals found in St Hilary a convenient and attractive location, suitably spacious residences and, for those so inclined, opportunities for hunting and shooting.

In 1909 the Beaupre estate was put up for sale and was described in the sale catalogue in suitably eulogistic tones. Here was a 'highly valuable, freehold, historical, residential and sporting estate' comprising some 500 acres of land in the parishes of St Hilary and Llanblethian. It included good farms let to excellent tenants, there was a modern residence [New Beaupre] and 'the interesting remains of Old Beaupre Castle'. Fishing and shooting rights attached to the estate, and the entire property generated an annual income in excess of £1000. But no established or would-be landed gentleman came forward to acquire this desirable property and all but a few small lots were withdrawn from the sale. The auctioneers blamed the taxation implications of Lloyd George's 'People's Budget' for the lack of competition in the bidding, but whatever the reason Beaupre was destined to remain in Basset possession until the 1930s.

56. The Cross, 1908.

57. St Hilary Railway Halt, *c.*1912.
(The female passenger is believed to be Miss Mary Nicholl of Merthyr Mawr.)

The sale catalogue had stretched historical fact beyond its limits in claiming that Beaupre had been in the possession of one family, the Bassets, since the Conquest. But set against such evocations of the historic and the picturesque were more practical, modern recommendations to attract the prospective purchaser—the proximity of good rail and road communications.

Originally intended for freight transport, the Cowbridge and Aberthaw Railway (opened in 1892) subsequently carried passengers and introduced steam railcars or 'motor cars'on the line. In 1905 a passenger platform or halt was provided at St Hilary, close to Old Beaupre, and this gave local people access not only to places along the line but also to the wider rail network. The halt was closed to passengers in 1920, in the same month that the first daily bus service between Cowbridge and Cardiff was inaugurated, but the Aberthaw branch line continued to carry passengers and to serve industries along its length until the 1930s. Only a grassy track and a stone bridge now survive to recall the days of rail transport in St Hilary.

Nineteenth and twentieth-century maps of St Hilary show a parish dotted with old mine workings, old lead shafts and quarries, most of them long disused. It is known that lead was mined in St Hilary in the late-eighteenth century on glebe lands belonging to the Llandaff Cathedral Chapter, and it is probable that the lead deposits in the parish had been mined in the Roman period. But throughout the centuries mining and quarrying had been on a small scale and had done little to deface the rural landscape.

Developments in transport and communications brought even the smallest communities into immediate contact with events in the wider world and heightened the impact of those events. St Hilary, like every other parish in the Vale, saw its young men march off to war in

58. St Hilary in the 1920s.
(Detail from Ordnance Survey map, Glamorgan sheet XLV; Crown copyright.)

59. New Beaupre House in use as a Red Cross Hospital during the First World War.

60. Glamorganshire Yeomanry monument.

1914-18, mourned those who did not return and rejoiced in the safe return of others. A memorial plaque in the church lychgate names those who did return home. Memorials within the church remember the fallen: Hugh T. Ackland-Allen, lieutenant lst Battalion Royal Welch Fusiliers, killed in action near Ypres, October 1914, aged twenty-one; George Gilbert Traherne, captain Royal Field Artillery, killed in action in France, August 1916, aged forty-nine, having survived service on the Indian Frontier and in the Boer War; and George Rees, sergeant 13th Welsh Regiment, killed in France in the last days of the War, aged twenty-six.

New Beaupre, like many other large houses in the county, was used as a military convalescent hospital during the Great War. Memories of the men treated there have now all but faded away, but a simple obelisk erected on St Hilary Down in 1922 to commemorate the men of the Glamorganshire Yeomanry still stands, an enduring and highly visible reminder of the cost of war.

On the eve of the First World War, and within a few years of the abortive sale of Beaupre, S. T. Saunderson put his St Hilary estate on the market. The property, which centred on the village and included The Manor, The Cross, The Bush inn, Coed Hills, Village and East Down farms, was described in glowing terms in the sale catalogue and was purchased as a whole, with the exception of The Manor, by the Cardiff shipowner Henry Radcliffe. The Manor was bought by Charles Ackland-Allen who had previously lived at The Cross as tenant, and the house remained in the possession of the Ackland-Allens and their descendants the Giles family until the 1960s.

Village life in the early years of the twentieth century.

The village school was closed in 1910 despite the determined efforts of the managers to retain it. So few children were attending the school that its closure could no longer be postponed, and henceforth the village children had to walk along the lanes and across the fields to the Llandough (Llanfair) school in the adjacent parish. The old schoolroom was put to other uses including that of Reading Room, but memories and photographs survive to recall parents and grandparents, aunts, uncles and cousins who were pupils there.

From its first home in Manor Cottage the post office moved to Tyr Eglwys (later Abbotswood) where the postmistress Catherine Rees and her family are still remembered. Catherine's husband John, by trade a mason, was the sub-postmaster and also served as parish clerk in the 1920s.

Church Farm in the 1920s was worked by members of the Howells family who still used the old circular sty for its intended purpose. And at this date the parish pound, opposite The Manor stables, still housed the occasional straying animal.

One well-remembered character of the 1920s is Mrs Mog Thomas who lived in the cottage adjoining the old schoolroom. Every week Mrs Thomas went into Cowbridge to buy sweets and halfpenny bars of chocolate which she then sold from open boxes in her front room to village children.

During the inter-war years the Mansel Hall was the scene of many a village social gathering. This long room above the coach house belonging to The Cottage was, during the lifetime of Sir Thomas Mansel Franklen and his wife, made available to the people of St Hilary and memory still recalls the pleasure of dances and parties held there.

61. Pageant in the grounds of The Manor, with Miss Dorothy Florence Ackland-Allen, *c.*1913.

62. Harvest time at East Down farm with members of the Davies family, *c.*1930.

63. The Grange (photographed 1998).

The 1920s and 1930s saw a succession of new families moving into the village, among them the Bruces from Lanelay, near Llantrisant. Sir Gerald Bruce, soldier, solicitor and lord lieutenant of the county, purchased The Vicarage from the Church in Wales in 1924 and the then vicar, the Reverend Lewis Crockett, and his family moved into The Cross which became the vicarage. Before bringing his family to St Hilary Sir Gerald extended his new property and renamed it The Grange.

Life at The Grange is recalled by Mrs Maud Jenkins (née Young) who as a young woman was house parlourmaid first at Lanelay and then at St Hilary. She was one of six house servants employed by the Bruces, her fellow servants being housemaid, 'between maid', cook, kitchenmaid and laundrymaid, plus a housekeeper and a children's governess. Maud and the others ate in the servants' hall and slept in attic rooms, working long hours especially when the Bruces entertained or returned home late at night. The staff were given two weeks holiday in the summer and for Maud this was an opportunity to visit her own family at Brynna. Outdoor staff employed at The Grange included a groom and a gardener, and Maud Jenkins vividly recalls the well-tended gardens, particularly the walled kitchen garden where a rich variety of fruit (including luscious strawberries all the more luscious for being picked surreptitiously) and vegetables was produced both out-of-doors and in heated greenhouses.

It was in the 1930s that the Staien family of Coed Hills stud farm became landowners in St Hilary, purchasing the Beaupre estate from the representatives of the Basset family in 1931 and acquiring a number of cottages in the village from the trustees of Wyndham Ivor Radcliffe the same year. In 1951 the Staiens handed Old Beaupre into the guardianship of the then Ministry of Works.

The long connection of the Traherne and Edmondes families with St Hilary was maintained well into the present century. The Cottage continued in Traherne ownership

64. Manor Cottage No. 2, with Mrs Elizabeth Eddolls and Mrs Mary Willis, *c.*1930.

65. Manor Cottage No. 1, with Bert and Dorcas Lassiter and family, *c.*1930.

66. Ted and Florrie Foreman's cottage (now site of Lansdowne) with Foreman children, 1930s.

after the death of John Montgomery Traherne in 1860 when the bulk of his St Hilary estate passed to the Saundersons. Harriet, wife of George Montgomery Traherne, enjoyed the property for life, and after her death in 1900 it passed to George Gilbert Traherne and his descendants. Not until 1939 did the Traherne family relinquish ownership of the house, the new owners being Mr and Mrs J. C. Clay. Ownership of The Lodge was retained by the Edmondes family until 1934 when the property was sold to Sir Gerald Bruce by Charles Thomas Edmondes, and Erw Faen was the home of Mrs D. C. Edmondes, wife of Charles Gresford Irving Edmondes, throughout her widowhood until her death in 1963.

67. Erection of Beacon on The Downs to celebrate the coronation of King George VI, 1937.
Figures left to right: Jonah Jones, gardener at the Grange; Richard Morgan, Village Farm; David Watts, mayor of Cowbridge; 2 unidentified; David Davies, East Down farm and his grandchild Mary.
The two men on the bonfire are Mary's father Tom Davies and 'Timber Tom'.

People and places later in the century

The name of Clay, like that of Radcliffe, is part of the commercial and shipping history of Cardiff and South Wales, but the name J. C. (Johnnie) Clay evokes memories in altogether different circles. Indeed, J. C. Clay has become a legend in cricketing history, for this was the man whose county cricketing career spanned over a quarter of a century, who captained Glamorgan from 1924-27 and again in 1946, who played for England and who established batting and bowling records that stood unchallenged for many years. Aged almost fifty, he was a member of the Glamorgan team when they won the county championship in 1948, having played a decisive role as batsman and bowler throughout the season. This man of quiet humour who died in 1973 would surely have appreciated the embellishment of his gravestone with a carved cricket ball. J. C. Clay's sporting interests also extended to horses and horse racing. In 1972 his horse *Charlie H* won the Welsh Grand National, and great were the celebrations in St Hilary in the wake of that event. At Chepstow Racecourse, where J. C. Clay was a director and steward, a long distance steeplechase, The J. C. Clay Memorial Chase, was established in his memory. And in St Hilary, the annual point-to-point, established in 1970, continues to enjoy the support of the Clay family.

68. J. C. (Johnnie) Clay (1898-1973), Glamorgan and England cricketer.

The inter-war years, the Second World War and the latter decades of the twentieth century have all contributed to the changing face of St Hilary. Superficially, that change is not evident. Stone cottages and houses still cluster around the church, maintaining the pattern of the nucleated village established in medieval times. There is a picturesque thatched inn, and an equally picturesque thatched cottage facing the village green. But beyond the picture postcard image the signs of recent change and development become apparent.

Once small thatched cottages have been demolished or transformed into substantial modern residences, and in a village where thatched roofs once predominated slates and tiles are now the norm. At the beginning of the twentieth century farming and allied rural trades dominated the life of village and parish. Today, while the farming tradition is continued by families such as the Thomases at The Farm and the Llewellyns at Old Beaupre, in the village itself evidence of an agricultural past is hard to find. Obsolete farm buildings—barns (including the old tithe barn), stables and cowsheds—have been converted into houses, most of whose occupants have no connection with farming. The parish pound, long used to confine straying animals, barely survives, the only clue to its existence a doorway in the stone boundary wall of Myrtle Cottage. The village smithy survives only in memory. The eighteenth-century circular pigsty still stands, but has been transformed into a decorative feature and now stands in splendid isolation in the garden of Church Cottage with not a pig in sight.

69. The circular pigsty (photographed 1998).

Post-war housing has done much to change the outward face of St Hilary. The village green is fringed by council houses built, in the 1950s, to house families from some of those picturesque but undeniably primitive cottages. Three of those cottages adjacent to the village hall rapidly became derelict and were demolished. One cottage-style property was built on the site by the new owners, using such stone as could be salvaged, and today Little Hall Cottage, with its stone walls, thatched roof and small windows, belies its recent history. Since the 1950s extensive private house building in the heart of the village and on its western edge has had a considerable impact upon the landscape. In 1891 there were just 36 houses in St Hilary, a number that remained unchanged until *c.*1950, and the population totalled 175. At the end of the twentieth century there were over 80 houses (85 in 1990) accommodating a population of some 260. More houses, bigger houses, smaller families and households, together with a wide range of professional and business occupations point to a community which has undergone profound social changes in the course of the twentieth century.

1913

1950s

1950s

1990s

70. The story of Little Hall Cottage.

71. Pill Box, a survival from the Second World War (photographed 1998).

The sale in 1961 of farms owned by the Radcliffe estate, including Coed Hills, East Down, Village and Garn, gave tenant farmers and others in St Hilary the opportunity to become land and property owners. Property sales also attracted purchasers from further afield, and while some newcomers put down roots others stayed only briefly, setting the pattern for an increasingly mobile population. Properties now change hands with a frequency unimaginable fifty years ago, and it is a telling indication of such change that only two of St Hilary's adult residents in 1999 were born in the parish and that only one of those has lived her entire life in St Hilary.

Despite all the changes of the twentieth century, St Hilary retains a certain timeless quality. There are the ruins of Old Beaupre (now in the care of CADW) with their power to evoke the glories of past centuries, the unspoilt rural landscape, the narrow lanes weaving their way through the village. Amidst such surroundings there stands, incongruously, a lone Pill Box, a relic of the Second World War. Built to guard one of the southern routes into the village, this austere, brick-built edifice adjacent to Village Farm is a reminder of measures taken in the Vale, as in the country at large, to counter the threat of German invasion. A second Pill Box, sited near Abbotswood to guard the approach from Old Beaupre, was demolished years ago.

In 1990 St Hilary celebrated its medieval origins with a whole series of events both 'medieval' and 'modern'. To celebrate the dawn of a new millennium the community added a new treble bell to the ring of five in the church tower. When all six bells rang out to welcome the year 2000 AD another chapter opened in the history of St Hilary.

72. 'St Hilary 900' celebrations, 1990. Medieval Fair Day and Tree-planting at The Clump.

POSTSCRIPT

In 1188 a distinguished band of travellers rode across Stalling Down within earshot of the small community of St Hilary. Some local people must have caught sight of the riders and been mightily impressed. For here was Archbishop Baldwin and his entourage hastening westward on their journey around Wales 'preaching the Cross' to recruit a crusader army. In that entourage was Gerald of Wales (Giraldus Cambrensis) who has left behind him a colourful account of his travels in his *Journey Through Wales*. Sadly, little attracted Gerald's attention as he and his companions rode from Llandaff to Margam, and of St Hilary and the other small communities close to the route there is not a mention.

In later centuries, as increasing numbers of antiquarians and travellers explored the Vale and compiled accounts of its topography and history, St Hilary merited little attention other than descriptions of Old Beaupre and of the de Cardiff and Basset tombs in the church. St Hilary's broader social history had, apparently, run an unexceptional and unrecorded course and left nothing beyond a few ancient monuments to illuminate the past.

What has been revealed during the research for this present publication is a colourful pattern of events and personalities in which the significant and the trivial fuse together to give form and character to the life of the place and its people. St Hilary has a rich past and its history is, above all else, that of families and individuals bound together by strong social and economic ties. Its story is, in many respects, a microcosm of that of the wider Vale, but it is also, uniquely, that of one vital community with its own distinctive identity

Arrival of the Millennium Bell, Ash Wednesday 1999.

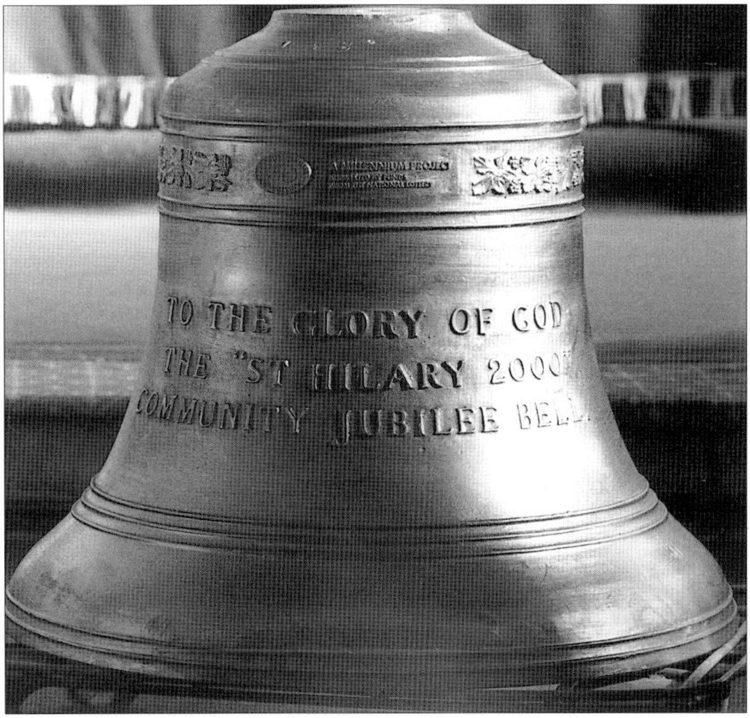

73. The St Hilary Millennium Bell dedicated by the Archbishop of Wales, 8 March 1999.

ACKNOWLEDGEMENTS

It was at the invitation of the 'St Hilary 2000' Committee that I undertook the work of researching and writing a history of St Hilary, and I would like to record my thanks to the members of that Committee for their support throughout the progress of the project.

Local knowledge is an invaluable asset for anyone investigating the history of a particular place. I have been singularly fortunate in the help I have received from present-day residents of St Hilary and from former residents who have maintained their links with the village, and I thank them all for sharing their knowledge with me.

I am especially grateful to Jeannie Griffiths, Elgiva Thomas, Stephen Williams and Elizabeth Giles. Sadly, Stephen did not live to see the publication of this history in which he had taken such a keen interest. His informed comments and gentle criticisms were generously given and gratefully received. He would be delighted to know that his son, Simon, designed the dust jacket of this book. I also thank Brian Ll. James for sharing his extensive knowledge of the Vale with me.

Members of staff in the following institutions are thanked for their assistance: Glamorgan Record Office, Cardiff; Cardiff Central Library; Bridgend Library (Coed Parc); National Library of Wales, Aberystwyth; National Museum & Gallery, Cardiff; Public Record Office, London (Genealogical Centre); CADW; Royal Commission on the Ancient and Historic Monuments of Wales.

The typing skills of Gillian Griffiths greatly facilitated the progress of this work, and I thank her also for the original sketches which enhance this publication.

The computer and graphics skills of the printers ensured that the printing process went smoothly, and I am grateful to Keith and Eurion Brown for their friendly help and advice.

The responsibility for any errors of fact or interpretation within these pages is entirely mine. I hope that they are few, and that all who read this book will do so with enjoyment.

Hilary M. Thomas

The following individuals are thanked for providing photographs and other pictorial items used as illustrations in this publication: Elgiva Thomas, Elizabeth Giles, Mike Kemp, Jeannie Griffiths, Roy Lassiter, Lorraine Ravey, Mary Thomas, Joan Davies and Nigel Anderson.

BRIEF GUIDE TO SOURCES

Cardiff. Glamorgan Record Office. St. Hilary parish records (P/12): parish registers, 1690 to date; parish accounts, 1728-1821; tithe award, 1839. Quarter Sessions records (Q/S). Estate and family collections: Aubrey (D/D Au); Edmondes (D/D Ed); Loveluck (D/D Lov); Dynevor (D/D D); Morgan Bruce (D/D MBN). Land Tax assessments, 1783-1831 (LTA Cow). Ordnance Survey maps, 1877 and subsequent editions .

Cardiff. Central Library. David Jones of Wallington manuscripts; Mansel Franklen photograph albums.

Cardiff. Church in Wales Offices. Ecclesiastical Commissioners Files and Queen Anne's Bounty files (EC L 126 and QAB L 126).

Aberystwyth. National Library of Wales. Mansel Franklen collection; Great Sessions files; Church in Wales records (Llandaff diocese), including Wills & Inventories and Visitation Returns.

Bridgend. Bridgend Library (Coed Parc). Microfilm copies of: Census Enumerators Returns, 1841-91 (also available in Glamorgan Record Office); Newspaper files, including *Western Mail.*

London. Public Record Office (Genealogical Centre). Wills proved in the Prerogative Court of Canterbury (PROB/11).

SHORT BIBLIOGRAPHY

Glamorgan County History (General Editor, Glanmor Williams): Vol. 111, *The Middle Ages,* ed. T. B. Pugh; Vol. IV, *Early Modern Glamorgan*, ed. Glanmor Williams (Cardiff, 1971, 1974).

The Royal Commisssion on Ancient and Historic Monuments in Wales. *An Inventory of the Ancient Monuments in Glamorgan.* Vol. IV. *Domestic Architecture from the Reformation to the Industrial Revolution. Part 1, The Greater Houses; Part 2, Farmhouses and Cottages* (HMSO 1981, 1988).

Nicholas Carlisle, *A Topographical Dictionary of Wales* (London, 1811).

G. T. Clark, *Cartae et alia munimenta quae ad dominium de Glamorgan pertinent,* 2nd edn, 6 vols. (Cardiff, 1910).

G. T. Clark, *Limbus Patrum Morganiae et Glamorganiae, being the genealogies of the older families of the lordships of Morgan and Glamorgan* (London, 1911).

G. T. Clark, 'The parish of St. Hilary, in Glamorganshire, and its Lords', *Archaeologia Cambrensis,* 1889.

G. T. Clark, 'Manorial Particulars of the County of Glamorgan', *Archaeologia Cambrensis,* 1878.

J. S. Corbett, *Glamorgan. Papers and Notes on the Lordship and its Members* (Cardiff, 1925).

Roy Denning (ed.), *The Diary of William Thomas, 1762-1795* (South Wales Record Society publication no. 11, 1995).

C. A. H. Green, *Notes on Churches in the Diocese of Llandaff* (Aberdare, 1906-7).

D. B. Hague, *Old Beaupre Castle, Glamorgan* (Official Guidebook, 1965).

Brian Ll. James, 'The Vale of Glamorgan, 1840-60. Profile of a Rural community', *Glamorgan Historian* Vol. V, ed. Stewart Williams (1968).

Brian Ll. James, 'The Welsh Language in the Vale of Glamorgan', *Morgannwg* XVI (1972).

Brian Ll. James and David J. Francis, *Cowbridge and Llanblethian Past and Present* (Cowbridge, 1979).

Samuel Lewis, *A Topographical Dictionary of Wales* (London, 1833).

Benjamin Heath Malkin, *The Scenery, Antiquities and Biography of South Wales* (London, 1804).

J. Hobson Matthews (ed.), *Cardiff Records, Material for a History of the County Borough,* 6 vols. (Cardiff, 1898-1911).

Rice Merrick, *Morganiae Archaiographia: A Book of the Antiquities of Glamorganshire,* ed. Brian Ll. James (South Wales Record Society publication no. 1, 1983).

J. H. Morgan, *The County Cricket Series: Glamorgan* (London, 1952).

Prys Morgan, *Iolo Morganwg* (Cardiff, 1975).

John Newman, *Glamorgan, Buildings of Wales Series,* vol. 3 (Penguin Books, 1995).

Thomas Nicholas, *The History and Antiquities of Glamorganshire and its families* (London, 1874).

Iltyd B. Nicholl, 'Report of the Cowbridge Meeting of the Cambrian Archaeological Association, August 1888', *Archaeologia Cambrensis,* 1888.

Geoffrey R. Orrin, *Medieval Churches of the Vale of Glamorgan* (Bridgend, 1988).

Elizabeth Parkinson (ed.), *The Glamorgan Hearth Tax Assessment of 1670* (South Wales Record Society publication no. 10, 1994).

William Rees, *Industry before the Industrial Revolution* (Cardiff, 1968).

D. G. Tucker, 'The Lead Mines of Glamorgan and Gwent', *Morgannwg* XX (1976).

Roderick G. Williams, 'Vale of Glamorgan Sketches, St. Hilary and Old Beaupre', *Aberafan and Margam District Historical Society Transactions,* vol. 3 (1930).

Stephen W. Williams, 'Some Monumental Effigies in Wales', *Archaeologia Cambrensis,* 1890.